The Complete Louisiana Catahoula Leopard Dog

Also by Don Abney

The Abney Method to Owning a Dog
Canine Tracking Guide
The Catahoula Leopard Dog
(out of print)

www.donabney.com

The Complete Louisiana Catahoula Leopard Dog

Don Abney

AuthorHouse™
1663 Liberty Drive
Bloomington, IN 47403
www.authorhouse.com
Phone: 1-800-839-8640

© *2011 Don Abney. All rights reserved.*

No part of this book may be reproduced, stored in a retrieval system, or transmitted by any means without the written permission of the author.

First published by AuthorHouse   3/25/2011

ISBN: 978-1-4567-5521-8 (e)
ISBN: 978-1-4567-5522-5 (dj)
ISBN: 978-1-4567-5523-2 (sc)

Library of Congress Control Number: 2011904878

Printed in the United States of America
Book and cover design by Church Road Books
Any people depicted in stock imagery provided by Thinkstock are models, and such images are being used for illustrative purposes only.
Certain stock imagery © Thinkstock.

This book is printed on acid-free paper.

Because of the dynamic nature of the Internet, any web addresses or links contained in this book may have changed since publication and may no longer be valid. The views expressed in this work are solely those of the author and do not necessarily reflect the views of the publisher, and the publisher hereby disclaims any responsibility for them.

Dedicated to the memory of
my Friend and Mentor
VERNON TRAXLER
1927 – 2011

To The Reader

This book is designed to provide brief information on the history, care, uses, and breeding of Louisiana Catahoula Leopard Dogs. It is sold with the understanding that the publisher and author are not providing veterinary, legal, accounting, or other professional advice.

It is not the purpose of this book to reprint all the information that is available from other authors and/or publishers, but instead to complement, amplify, and supplement other texts. You are urged to read all the available material and tailor the information to your individual needs.

Every effort has been made to make the information contained in this work as complete and as accurate as possible at the time of publication. However, there may be mistakes, both typographical and in content. Therefore, this text should be used only as a general guide and not as the ultimate source for owning or breeding Catahoulas.

The purpose of this work is to educate the reader, based on my experiences owning and breeding Catahoulas. The author and his associates have neither liability nor responsibility to any person or entity with respect to any loss or damage caused, or alleged to have been caused, directly or indirectly, by any information contained in or omitted from this book.

Table of Contents

Preface . . . . *xi*
Acknowledgements . . . . *xiii*
Introduction . . . . *xv*
History 1
A Dog of Distinction 15
Conformation Standard 21
Genetically Speaking 29
Coat 35
Eyes 41
Deafness 45
Hips 51
Parasites 57
Diseases and Vaccines 73
Facts About Food 79
General Care 95
Catahoulas at Work and Play 101
Selecting The Breeding Pair 113
Understanding The Heat Cycle 121
Breeding Age and Frequency 125
Breeding Styles 131
Breeding Methods 135
The Breeding 139
Pregnancy – Care and Feeding 143
Whelping 147
Post Delivery 151
Reproduction Problems 157
Unplanned Breeding 161
Afterword *163*
About the Author *165*
Bibliography *169*

Preface

I have loved and owned Catahoulas for most of my adult life, and believe that there is no finer canine on the planet. There are many breeds that claim to be versatile, but the Catahoula does not only state the claim, it proves it.

Knowing what is in the dog is just as important as what is on the outside; genetics versus aesthetics. Through the help of many dedicated breeders and researchers, I have learned a great deal about the genetic composition of the Catahoula and the importance of structure, movement, ability, temperament, and drive. I have had the privilege of being included in the results of genetic studies performed by scientists who added the Catahoula to their research projects. This book contains information and techniques that I have used to help produce quality working, hunting, and conformation champion Catahoulas. It is my hope that this information will increase your knowledge of the Louisiana Catahoula Leopard Dog and aid you in becoming a better breeder and owner.

Acknowledgments

Through the course of compiling the history of the Catahoula, I met some very interesting people and heard many intriguing facts and stories. Thanks to all of you for providing information, pictures, support, and friendship needed to complete this work.

To those members of the Wright, McMillin, and Fairbanks families, thank you for sharing your lives and family history with me. Without all of you, this work would not have been possible.

Abney, Kathleen, Abney Catahoulas, LA
Aden, Aubrey, Aden Catahoulas, Carriere, MI
Bickel, Ja'Na, The Woodlands, TX
Booth, Kimberly (Fairbanks heir), Ferriday, LA
Bumgarner, Carl, California
Collins (Fairbanks), Myrtle Ann (Lovie Fairbanks' granddaughter), Jonesville, LA
Corlew, Charles "Tony," Corlew Catahoulas, Carrolton, GA
Caldwell, Eleanor, Language Department, School of Choctaw Language, Choctaw Nation of Oklahoma
Fields, K.T. "Hutke," Great Sun, Chief, Natchez Nation, Gore, OK
Gregory, Hiram F. "Pete," PhD, professor of anthropology, Northwestern State University, Natchitoches, LA
Labranche, Gregory, DVM, Covington, LA
Lake, Sandra, Evangeline Catahoulas, Ontario, Canada
Leggio, Andrea, Wappingers Falls, NY
McMillin, Leroy (Talbot A. McMillin's great-grandson), Spring, TX
Ott, Nicole, Double Ott Catahoulas, Franklin, LA
Walsh-Bunny, Stephanie, Jetta Catahoulas, Indianapolis, IA
White, Suzanne, Tumbling Run Catahoulas, Mt. Holly Springs, PA
Wright, John Preston (Lankford Preston Wright's grandson), Texas City, TX

Introduction

The Louisiana Catahoula Leopard Dog is not your everyday, run-of-the-mill mongrel, but a dog that has been developed through both chance breeding and controlled breeding. These have provided satisfaction to those in need of a dog to perform a job or give companionship and enjoyment to anyone owning these spectacular dogs. The Catahoula has evolved from a line of Cur Dogs into one of the most recognized working dogs in the South, and is proving itself in many of the various ring sports.

As I have often stated, this is a dog that needs to be exercised, rain or shine, because, if he is confined for too long a period of time, he will eat your house. If you are looking for a dog that will sit and watch television with you, this is not the dog for you.

The Catahoula is more closely related to the Red Wolf and the Village Dog than most of the breeds that are available today. In the history of the Catahoula, I have provided information that will contradict some of the previous teachings about the breed. Their history is clouded and very difficult to follow, but I have placed before the reader the information I have found through years of research. It is up to readers to draw their own conclusion as to its inception.

There are differing opinions concerning a working dog versus a show dog. Opinions aside, the breed standard for working, hunting, and herding breeds was established by owners and breeders of those dogs that performed the jobs for which they were intended. The breed standard includes a short history of the breed, the general appearance, and a description of the individual parts of the dog's structure and movement. In other words, the breed standard describes a perfect specimen. It is worth mentioning here that the perfect specimen does not exist. As much as everyone wishes to believe they have the perfect dog, every dog has a flaw. Your job as a breeder is to identify those flaws and choose a mate that will help to correct or eliminate them. Always "breed up" in your attempts to produce the perfect dog. "Breeding up" is a term used for introducing a mate that is better than the dog you intend to breed.

Most ranchers and hunters want a dog that will do the job they need accomplished, regardless of its appearance. The uninformed look upon conformation shows as a beauty pageant, where dogs are paraded around a ring and chosen only for their appearance. In fact, conformation shows are designed to allow a qualified judge to examine a dog, both visually and physically, for proper structure and movement, in accordance with the written breed standard. What is often overlooked is that the written standard that governs conformation shows is the same standard that was devised by the owners of working dogs. Two major components, structure and movement, are what enable the working dog to perform its job more efficiently and effortlessly.

When speaking with those persons using a working dog, opinions will vary, but for the most part it is considered a dog that herds, hunts, or bays game. The dictionary defines work as "a productive or operative activity." This definition would imply that a true working dog is one that has the ability to perform a specific function for which it is trained. This includes herding, hunting, treeing, guarding, tracking, therapy and assistance, or locating a specific scent source, such as those used in search and rescue, cadaver, arson, and narcotics and bomb detection, as well as locating or tracking animals.

Desire, or prey drive, is another specific aspect of the working dog, and is more often displayed in field trials. Desire is the motivator that drives a dog to perform an intended function. Without desire, the dog will not perform this intended function to the best of his ability. Individuals using their dogs for working purposes do not have the time, patience, or inclination to feed a dog that does not earn his keep, or perform the function for which it was intended.

Breeders of working, herding, and hunting breeds should concentrate on creating a total package when developing their line of dog. Drive, temperament, structure, and movement are equally important components of the working dog, and breeders must strive to maintain them. This is also true for breeders of conformation, obedience, and competition dogs, as well as those used in ring sports. Ignoring the working aspects of the breed for the purpose of producing a "pretty" dog would lead to the development of an inferior representation of the breed.

 # History

IN the early 1500s, the Indians in and around Louisiana used the Red Wolf's cunning ability to aid them in locating game much in the same manner as modern-day hunters use their dogs. The wolves, though wild, would maintain a safe distance at the outskirts of the Indian camps in search of food that might be left behind. By tossing scraps of food to the wolves, a bond was established, enabling the Indians to use the wolf's expertise and tracking ability in the pursuit of game. By forming this bond with the wolves, the Indians were able to hunt within the same vicinity as the wolf packs without concern of having their position exposed and, ultimately, scaring off the game.

The American Indians could be perceived as the original naturalists. Primitive in their lifestyle as compared to that of the explorers to come, the Indians were nomadic, moving with the herds of animals and changes in weather, and never claiming the land on which they lived. The Indians would not kill an animal for the sport of killing, but would do so for food to support the village or to defend against an attack. The pelts or skins of the animals were used to fashion clothing, so there was very little waste.

There are some historians who point to breeds other than those carried by DeSoto as being a part of the Catahoula's inception. Some of the breeds mentioned are Xoloitzcuintli, Peruvian Inca Orchid, and Carolina Dog. I offer the following information.

The Xoloitzcuintli is a small dog native to Mexico and Central and South America. It is similar in appearance to the Pharaoh Hound and known to be the dog of the Aztecs. This breed ranges in size from nine to 30 pounds. In addition to its small stature, this breed is known for the dominant trait of hairlessness and has upright ears. Although considered an ancient breed, it could not have endured the winters of northern Louisiana.

The Peruvian Inca Orchid originated in Peru and lived in the homes of the Inca nobility, as was discovered by Spanish explorers in the early 1500s. This places a very limited timeline on its appearance in Louisiana or of being any part of the Catahoula's heritage. There is no record of Spanish explorers carrying any of these dogs to North America during the period of the Catahoula's inception. Since this was the dog of Inca nobility, why would they place their dogs in the hands of conquistadors? Another important note is that the Peruvian Inca Orchid also carries the dominant trait of hairlessness and has upright ears.

The Carolina Dog, which was located in Georgia and South Carolina, has some distinctions of its own.
1. Females annually have three heat cycles in rapid succession.
2. They regurgitate food for their offspring.
3. They have upright ears.
4. They are very social by nature. The Carolina Dog adapts easily with other dogs and looks on older dogs as being the alpha, and will submit to their will.
5. It is widely believed that these dogs crossed over from the Bering Strait during the time prior to the melting glaciers. Experts have stated that it is doubtful that migration across the Strait at that time would have been impossible without the use of sled dogs.
6. The senior research ecologist at the University of Georgia's Savannah River Ecology Lab, Dr. I. Lehr Brisbin, Jr., found in his skull study that there was a resemblance between 2000-year-old skulls and those of the Carolina Dog. He concluded that the differences were too large to prove any connection between the two.

From my research, there have never been any reported incidents of a "hairless Catahoula," or one with "upright ears." Because hairlessness is a dominant trait, someone throughout the years should have reported a Catahoula that was born hairless or with upright ears.

Geologists uncovered an ancient grave in Jonesville, Louisiana, in which a dog had been buried along with its owner. Killing and burying the dog along with the owner was an ancient tradition. There were some Catahoula historians that jumped to the conclusion that since this was an ancient ruin, the dog had to be one of those identifiable ancient breeds. Unfortunately, the animal has never been identified. It has been confirmed from skull measurements that the animal is neither a wolf nor a Catahoula, nor is it any of the known and identifiable breeds.

In her lecture to the World Small Animal Veterinary Association in 2005, Susan Janet Crockford, PhD., of Pacific Identifications, Inc., Victoria, BC, Canada, brought up the issue of domestic dogs existing on the northwest coast of North America over 4000 years ago. There are many interesting points in her lecture, but I will cite only those that are germane to the Catahoula research.

Dr. Crockford stated that a dog known as the Wool Dog existed on the northwest coast about 4000 years ago. It is believed that this dog was brought to North America by ancient settlers. The Wool Dog was a small dog that could be compared to the modern Spitz, and its hair was used to weave blankets. In addition to the Wool Dog was a dog known as the Village Dog. It was taller than the Wool Dog and had a much shorter coat. Because the shorter coat is dominant, any mixing of the two resulted in dogs with shorter coats. This was not desirable to the people, so the Wool Dogs were placed on an island where they could breed only with each other and without any outside interference from the Village Dog. The Village Dog, because of its shorter coat, began its migration to the warmer climate of the south. It is strongly believed that the dogs buried in ancient graves are Village Dogs.

Could it be that the Village Dog is a part of the Catahoula? Keep in mind that wolves are not fond of dogs and a pack of wolves will kill a dog. However, the possibility exists that Village Dogs in heat could have been bred by a lone Red Wolf, thus creating another breed of canine. Could the Village Dog have become extinct because of the Red Wolf population? it is quite possible, but no one will ever know.

In their book *Wolves of North America*, Young and Goldman write: "During the 1800s, gray wolves ranged over the North American continent as far south as central Mexico. They did not inhabit the southeastern states, extreme western California, or far western Mexico. Red wolves originally appeared from central Texas to Florida and north to the Carolinas, Kentucky, southern Illinois, and southern Missouri."

In the *American Midland Naturalist*, published by the University of Notre Dame, the article "The Status of Wild Canis in Louisiana" by John W. Goertz, Larry V. Fitzgerald, and Ronald M. Nowak, 1975, describes a comparison study of 155 wolf skulls prior to 1963. It proved that the only wild canis found in Louisiana was the Red Wolf and that it was prolific in the state until around 1941. The first coyote trapping in Louisiana was not reported until 1949 from Vernon Parish. Furthermore, this study indicates that the coyote and extirpation by man were the reasons that the Red Wolf was pushed out of Louisiana. Additionally, the period from 1954 to 1963 exhibited the presence of the Red Wolf in Louisiana, but in very limited numbers.

The Spanish explorer Hernando DeSoto, along with 10 ships containing a thousand soldiers, explorers, priests, and their supplies, set sail from Cuba and landed in Florida in 1539. DeSoto also carried with him the dogs that have become known as War Dogs. These breeds were the Greyhound and Alano Mastiff of Spain. The next four years were spent exploring the southeastern United States from Florida to Louisiana in search of gold and treasure. During his travels, DeSoto encountered many tribes of Indians, most of which he battled in an effort to gain knowledge of their hidden treasure. The Alano has a reputation of being able to pull down very large game and holding on to it with ease. During his quests, DeSoto would use their abilities in battles with the Indians and as a means of torturing his captives. This was done by chaining a prisoner to a tree and allowing the dogs to attack him.

After suffering defeat in one of his later battles in Louisiana, DeSoto succumbed to his wounds in the Indian village of Guahoya on May 21, 1542, and was buried in the Mississippi River, reportedly in full armor. His remains have never been located. The remaining soldiers abandoned the dogs and began their trek southward, toward Texas, in an effort to return to Spain.

On being abandoned to fend for themselves, DeSoto's dogs roamed freely throughout Louisiana, as did the Red Wolf. The Indians treated the dogs in the same manner as they had the wolves. The dogs bred and interbred freely with each another and, because scientific studies prove prominent numbers of Red Wolves in Louisiana during this period, it is firmly believed that they are a part of the Catahoula's inception.

The offspring of the various breedings were then used by the Indians in the same manner as they had used the wolves. On his return from an expedition to Louisiana circa 1683, Henri de Tonti (Iron Hand), an Italian explorer, gave a description of the strange-looking dogs he had seen while on his journey. He referred to these dogs as "Wolf Dogs," and said they possessed "haunting white eyes." He told how the Indians were able to use the dog's abilities to track and retrieve game from the swamps of Louisiana.

In 1699, an unknown Taensa Indian presented Iberville with a list of villages that existed in the area at that time. Those villages were Taensas, Chaoucoula, Conchayon, Couthaougoula, Nyhougoulas, Ohytoucoulas, and Talaspa, all of which are connected to the Muskogean family.

After the slaughter of the Natchez Indians by the order of Governor Jean-Baptiste Le Moyne de Bienville in 1733, tribal members from four different tribes joined together. They settled in the area where the Red, Black, and Little rivers come together in Jonesville, Louisiana. The people joining there came from the Avoyelle (also known as Little Taensa), Tunica, Ofo, and Choctaw tribes, who lived peacefully together on the outer areas of the fort, without interference from the French.

Although American history shows no account of a tribe known as the Catahoula Indians to exist, there is a reference of this tribe's existence in the history kept by the Natchez and Choctaw Indians. In an interview with the Natchez Nation's Principal Peace Chief, K. T. "Hutke" Fields, Great Sun, he states that there is a great deal of Indian history that is left out of American history books. It is their belief that the group that formed near the fort became known as the Catahoula Indians.

The languages spoken by the Tunica, Ofo, Avoyelle, Taensas, and Choctaw, as well as other tribes of the area, are varying dialects of Muskogean, so it is easy to see how the languages would have blended together. Chief Fields stated that the Ofo, Tunica, Avoyelle, Taensa, and the group identified as the Catahoula are all recognized and considered cousins of the Natchez Indians. The below list are all considered cousins to the Natchez Indians:

- Atakapa
- Avoyel

- Bidai
- Catahoula
- Chitimacha
- Opelousa
- Taensa
- Tunica

Considering the fact that four different Indian groups had combined, it is believed that this group, being content with their way of life, were known as the Catahoula Indians. In all likelihood, the Indian group and their dogs were identified by the same name, and it was meant as an insult.

There are conflicting theories of how the Catahoula Cur got its name. Some people theorize that the name Catahoula means "beloved lake," "clear lake," "clear water," "beautiful clear lake," or "clear eyes." The following is a translation of English to as provided by Eleanor Caldwell, Language Department, Choctaw Nation of Oklahoma, and *The Dictionary of the Choctaw Language* (1915) by Cyrus Byington.

Beautiful – aiukli, mismiki
Beloved – haloka, holitopa
Clear – hanta, masheli, okshauanli, okshauashli, shahbi, shohkalali, tohchalali
Danger – aleka, hepulla
Eye – chiluk, nishkin
Lake – haiyip, hohtak, okhata
River – bok, chuli, hacha, okhina
Water – fichak, oka, okchi, okchushba, okhata

In the Indian languages, when describing an object, the descriptive adjective should be placed after the object, or noun, which is reverse of the English language. Thus, in English, a description would appear as "Beautiful Lake," but in the Indian languages, it would be "Lake Beautiful." Knowing this, I present the following phrases with their Choctaw interpretation:

Beloved Lake – okhata aiukli
Clear Lake – okhata hanta
Clear Water – oka hanta

Beautiful Clear Lake – okhata hanta aiukli
Clear Eyes – nishkin hanta

Note that the Choctaw word "aiukli" is used to describe both "beloved" and "beautiful." Many Indian words have a double meaning and various spellings, and are dependent on the way they are used in a sentence. The distinction of spelling and/or meaning is in its application, and you must be familiar with the language in order to understand its use.

When viewing Indian writing, the letter "v" is a substitute for the English letter "a" and is pronounced "ah." As you can see from the above translations, the surmised myths relating Choctaw phrases to the pronunciation of the word "Catahoula" do not closely resemble any spellings or similarity in their use.

The Taensa Indians were members of the Natchez (pronounced "Not-Chay") Nation, but had separated from the tribe prior to the massacre of the Natchez Indians by Governor Bienville. The language of the Natchez is Muskogean, and since the Taensa were part of the Natchez at one time, their language would have been Muskogean also. Chief Fields provided information indicating that there may have been small changes in some word spellings, but the language of the Taensa remained very similar to that of the Natchez. The phrase "big, clear lake" would appear as "ahaya shel kahe e'a" (pronounced "ah ha ya-shail-kahay-ay-ah") when spoken in Muskogean (Taensa).

The Avoyelle Indians, sometimes spelled Avoy or Avoyel, were often referred to as the "Little Taensa" and were relatives of the Taensa Indians. This tribe was formed by members of the Taensa who split from the tribe and struck out on their own. Since they were relatives of the Taensa and Natchez Indians, their language would also have been Muskogean. There is no record of the Avoyelle language.

In his book *The History of the Choctaw, Chickasaw, and Natchez Indians*, H. B. Cushman provides a translation of the Muskogee word "Couthaougoula" (Coot-ha-oo-goo-la), as meaning "Choctaw." This word would have had frequent use by other tribal members in identifying the Choctaw Indians at Jonesville, Louisiana. Due to the close proximity, varying dialects, and the intermingling of the tribes, I believe that the word "Couthaougoula" was mispronounced, or slurred, by the French settlers when identifying the group of Indians in their vicinity, and the word came to be "Catahoula."

There are still other breeder/historians who presume the dog was named after Catahoula Parish in Louisiana. However, the dog had been evolving and recognized since the mid 1700s, but Catahoula Parish did not come to be known by this name until 1808. This leaves a great deal of doubt that the dog was named after the parish. Prior to its incorporation, Catahoula Parish was part of the original Concordia Parish granted to Jim and Rezin Bowie by Spain. In the history of Catahoula Parish, there is a belief that the name came from the Taensa Indian word "catoola," meaning "big, clear lake." Unfortunately, there is no known record of the Taensa language, but knowing that the Taensa were a group that split from the Natchez, the language would have been the same, or extremely similar. Additionally, one could make the case that the word "catoola" is simply another corruption of "Couthaougoula."

When studying the topographical maps of Louisiana, 1828–1882, the name Catahoula is spelled Catahoola. The "oo" spelling appears in 1828, 1855, and 1864, but when the same areas are examined on Louisiana maps dated 1835, 1856, 1874, and 1882, the name is spelled with "ou." This is a clear indication of spelling changes made by the composers, mostly French, as well as displaying a variance of reference materials used.

Further discussions with Chief Fields about the word "Catahoula" brought about this response. If the word Catahoula were spelled out using the Natchez alphabet (Muskogee), it would appear as "Ketehoulv." He agrees that the name "Catahoula," in all likelihood, was the mispronunciation or corruption of the word "Couthaougoula," and pointed out that Indian words with the letters "ou" together are unique to the Natchez language.

There are further references stating that the name Catahoula came from the Indian phrase "oka hullo," and has been translated to mean "beautiful lake." There is a river by that name appearing on a 1574 topographical map of Louisiana/Mississippi. Translating from Choctaw to English, the word "oka" means "water," and the word "hullo," also spelled "hollo," means (1) to put on, as in putting on shoes; or (2) to have a monthly flow, as in female menses. Given the fact that Indians used descriptive names based on appearance or characteristics, and knowing this to be a fierce, dangerous waterway, it is reasonable to believe that they would have named the river for its ferocity and not a woman's monthly cycle. The Choctaw word for danger is "hepulla," and it is reasonable to assume that they may have referred to this river as "oka hepulla." It has been proven that the French would apply what they heard phonetically from the manner in which it was pronounced by the Indians. They placed names on their maps in the manner in which they were heard and not exactly as meant by the Indians, resulting in many spellings and/or interpretations being changed. It is my belief that the river was named "oka hepulla," but was corrupted by the French to become "oka hulla," and then changed again to read "oka hullo."

So many incorrect identifications, interpretations, and translations were made by the early settlers, and the loss of many Indian languages, leaves us with a multitude of speculations. You will have to decide which explanation is more likely to have occurred. I maintain that the Catahoula got its name from the corruption of "Couthaougoula."

By the mid 1700s the French were more established in Louisiana and knowing of Tonti's reports of the abundance of game, they brought a dog from their country known as Bas Rouge, meaning Red Stockings. The Bas Rouge is also known as the Berger de Beauce, or more commonly, Beauceron. Seeing the way the Indians utilized their dog's abilities, the French began breeding the Beauceron with the wolf dog. It is worth mentioning at this time that the Beauceron is recognized in two colors, black with red stockings, and a three-colored merle of gray, black, and required tan trim.

Continuing with the evolution of the Catahoula, the French began breeding their Beauceron with the Wolf Dog in an effort to create a better dog that could work within the swamps. These breedings contributed to the inception of the dog that became known as the Catahoula Cur.

With the increase of civilization and population in the mid 1800s, purposeful and planned breedings by the settlers began to produce a dog that could work, hunt, guard, and occupy the children, all with a single dog. Thankfully, today we have the privilege of using information gleaned from years of breeding these dogs by people who have been commonly referred to as "Old-Timers." Their stories tell of what a great hunting and companion dog the Catahoula had become. Unfortunately, most of what we have are stories and information passed on by word of mouth. There were not many records kept of which breeding took place, or the method of doing so. Some of them had written down on paper which dogs were bred and to whom, but there are not many of those around. I was fortunate in finding a few of those scraps of paper.

The Catahoula, along with a few other breeds of dog, are referred to as the most versatile dog in the world. I cannot speak for all the other breeds, but I can identify with the versatility of the Catahoula. The following relates to how the Catahoula became the versatile dog that it is, and why those older breeders and hunters took such a hard stand about their dogs and litters. Their position was so firm that the only way you could acquire a Catahoula was to have someone give it to you. Catahoulas were never sold, and were only used by those who needed them for hunting or other types of work. It was believed that paying for a dog was a sin comparable to paying for the services of a prostitute.

I am sure that the following information will have some of you thinking that the practices used were cruel. Try to keep an open mind when reading this and understand their reasoning for using such practices. I wish to thank all of those who took the time to relate this to me and give me the opportunity to tell their side of what actually took place, and why. It is with their permission that I tell this piece of history.

In earlier years, money was very hard to earn. Most families not only worked at a full-time job, but generally worked on the farms of others, as well as their own farms, just to make ends meet and put food on their tables. The family dog was not just a pet as we know it today. If it did not work or perform some function in the day-to-day farm life, it was considered frivolous and was not kept for very long. It cost money to feed a dog, and if it did not earn its keep, it could not stay.

Those who used dogs to hunt or herd cattle would also use them to help with chores and protection. Breeding was only practiced to replace the dogs that were lost during a hunt, improve the dogs they owned, or traded for other things that were needed. White puppies, or puppies displaying a majority of white, were destroyed shortly after birth, as most of these puppies were believed to be deaf or deficient in some way. In their opinion, there was no reason to raise a dog that you would eventually have to shoot. The remaining puppies in the litter would be allowed to live until it was time to face another test.

There was a method used by hunters and ranchers that was effective in producing the best dogs. That method, if it were used today, would bring outcries of cruelty from animal rights groups. The method of culling for the best dogs was called "Lining."

Lining required the owner to bring an entire litter of pups, approximately 6 months of age, to a location where game or stock had been crossing. The dogs would be enticed to "take up the track," and would be released as a pack. The last two dogs to cross the line were shot by the owner. The reasoning was that the dogs did not show enough grit, or interest, in doing their job. The rest of the litter was allowed to go about tracking the scent. Upon their return, the first two to arrive were also shot. The reasoning here was that they did not show enough interest in the job to remain on the hunt with the pack. Those dogs that stayed on track and/or bayed-up showed the most promise, and were raised for working/hunting and generally became the next generation of breeding stock. This practice continued from litter to litter to ensure that only the best dogs were kept for hunting, working, and breeding. In those days, hunting was not just a sport, but a means of putting food on the table. Working a ranch dog meant not having to pay someone to help with locating, rounding up, or herding livestock. It did not make any sense to keep and feed a dog that did not do the job and do it well.

What makes the Catahoula so versatile? The answer is that these dogs were lined so hard that only the best of the best remained, bringing forth a strong, reliable, versatile dog. It is sad that some good dogs may have been destroyed by this method, but it only improved the working and hunting lines of dogs that remained. It may be hard to understand their reasoning, but they did the best they could with what they had, and it worked for them at that time. We have since learned that there are alternative methods to improving the quality of a dog.

An article printed in the *Concordia Sentinel* on July 19, 1979, by R. T. Bonnette, contained the announcement that the Catahoula Cur would be known as the Louisiana Catahoula Leopard Dog, and that a bill had been passed and signed by Governor Edwin Edwards making it the State Dog of Louisiana on July 9, 1979. Also mentioned in the article were Preston Wright, T. A. McMillin, and Lovie Fairbanks. Their inclusion in the article was to distinguish the three versions of Catahoula, which varied in size and color. Many hours have been spent locating the heirs of these men and acquiring information about them and their dogs.

The following information was confirmed by John Preston Wright, grandson of Lankford Preston Wright:

Lankford Preston Wright (1863–1940), commonly referred to as Preston, raised the largest of the Catahoulas, which displayed the brindle markings of De Soto's War Dogs. It was believed that these were the best working dogs in the area, the average weight of which was between 90 and 110 pounds. Preston told stories to his grandchildren about his having a Catahoula as his babysitter. There are newspaper articles with pictures of Preston Wright and Lovie Fairbanks, chronicling their Catahoulas and the black bear hunts in Cocodrie Swamp. There is also a story telling of how Preston and Lovie used their dogs to drive hogs from Harrisonburg, Louisiana, to Natchez, Mississippi, in the early 1900s without losing a single hog. This is a trek of approximately 40 miles as the crow flies, including crossing the Mississippi River, approximately one mile wide, by steam ferry from Vidalia, Louisiana, to Natchez, Mississippi.

John Wright states: "I can confirm that his (Preston Wright's) dogs were bred with red wolves from many stories that my dad and several uncles told me. My dad had several wolves as pets as a young boy, and in fact, we went to several old dens when I was a boy to see if we could capture any so I could try to raise one also. He would keep the wolves until they were approximately two years old, and then he would release them."

The following is from an interview with Leroy McMillin, great-grandson of T. A. McMillin:

"Talbot A. McMillin (1849–1919), who was born in Caddo Parish, Louisiana, and lived on Sandy Lake, raised mostly Blue Leopard dogs with glass eyes. It was said that his dogs were the best trailers, and their average weight was between 50 and 60 pounds. As a youth, I spent most summers on the family farm near Sandy Lake in Catahoula Parish. Naturally, anyone who had a farm back in those days had at least one dog, and chances were it was a Catahoula. The ones I remember were glass-eyed and smarter than most humans."

The following information comes from the Fairbanks family historian, Ms. Myrtle Ann (Fairbanks) Collins: "William Sullivan (Lovie) Fairbanks was born October 31, 1874, and died September 18, 1930. Lovie Fairbanks was a backyard veterinarian who traveled wherever he was needed to care for horses and other animals. He used his dog on bear, hogs, and wounded deer. Lovie kept a black bear in his home that used to eat at the kitchen table with him. His line of dogs varied in color from brindle to yellow, and was estimated to weigh between 65 and 75 pounds." It was reported that Lovie also kept a few Blue Leopard Catahoulas. He and Preston Wright lived within walking distance of one another, and both lived on the property previously owned by Jim and Rezin Bowie. This property has never changed owners and is still owned by the Fairbanks and Wright estates. Ms. Collins still resides on this property today.

With the passing of these three breeders and with the beginning of dog farming in the 1940s, the three individual lines have been lost due to crossing and interbreeding. It is speculated that the mixing of the three lines was for the purpose of producing a stronger, more colorful, and better working dog. This mixture of each of the lines explains why there is so much variation in size and color, even within the same litter. There are a few breeders who attempt to maintain the larger lines, but it has been established that the medium-sized Catahoula can endure the rigors of working far better than the larger line. Still, there are some hunters who prefer those dogs with a broader build, especially when it comes to bringing in a large boar. Ranchers, however, prefer the slimmer built and smaller-statured dogs.

The first registry to recognize the Catahoula as a pedigree was the Animal Research Foundation of Quinlan, Texas, in 1951, which was owned and operated by Mr. Tom D. Stodghill. By 1983, there were over 7800 Catahoulas registered. ARF is still registering dogs and is maintained by his daughter and her husband, Al Walker.

The National Association of Louisiana Catahoulas was formed on October 10, 1977, by Betty Anne Eaves, with the intent to register only purebred Catahoulas. The official standard of this organization was not produced until 1984 and has had little change since its inception. Ms. Eaves is credited with pursuing the recognition of the Catahoula as the State Dog. On July 9, 1979, the Catahoula Cur was officially named the Louisiana Catahoula Leopard Dog by Governor Edwin Edwards, and became the State Dog of Louisiana. There were other breeds of dogs so recommended, but the Catahoula, because of its inception in Louisiana, was presented with the distinction of being the State Dog.

The United Kennel Club recognized the Louisiana Catahoula Leopard Dog on January 1, 1995. The standard used by UKC was the same as that of NALC until the UKC-registered breeders stood together to make changes that were more in line with current genetic facts and findings. In January 2008, the UKC standard was again changed to include the natural bob-tailed specimens. UKC will accept NALC registrations into their registry.

Most Catahoulas are born with a long tail, but there are some that are born with a naturally shorter tail. Genetically shorter-tailed specimens are acceptable within most registries and are referred to as Bob-Tailed Catahoulas. Surgically shortening the tail is not approved or accepted.

The Catahoula was added to the American Kennel Club as a herding breed in 2010. Most breeders do not wish to be affiliated with this organization. Their main reason is the AKC's habitual changing of breed standards to suit design instead of function.

I have placed before you the facts as I know them, gleaned from years of research on the Catahoula's inception. What is the true make-up of the Catahoula? You will have to form your own conclusions. Due to the loss of so much history, the true inception of the Catahoula may never be known. Just remember this: Regardless of where the Catahoula came from or how it came to be, we have been presented with a dog that can perform any task. It is our responsibility as breeders to preserve this breed.

A Catahoula will perform any task, regardless of the difficulty, for there is no limit to its versatility.

 A Dog of Distinction

WHENEVER I am asked what makes a Catahoula so much different from other breeds, my answer is "versatility and uniqueness." This is truly one of the most versatile dogs ever to exist. This breed is comfortable with working in virtually any arena. By "working," I refer to any type of work where the use of a dog would be desirable. Catahoulas provide assistance in all aspects of herding, hunting, service assistance, search and rescue, body recovery, tracking, arson, narcotics, and explosives detection. It is unique not only in the variations of its coat and eye color, but in its ability to adapt to almost any situation. Their behavior may range from clownish when relaxing with their family to very serious and assertive when performing their duty.

When it comes to work, the Catahoula is unsurpassed in its concentration on performing its job. Most herding dogs herd in a manner known as Heeling. Heeling is the act of nipping at the heels of an animal and forcing it to move in a chosen direction. The method of herding performed by the Catahoula is known as Heading. Heading places the dog at the head of an animal or herd, where it will lead them in a desired direction. If an animal decides it is not going in that direction, the Catahoula will bark and bite at the face of the animal, forcing it to move in the proper direction. There are times when an animal will refuse to move and make a stand in defiance. When this occurs, the Catahoula will bark and agitate the animal until it moves. This usually results in the animal charging the Catahoula, whereby the Catahoula will simply trot off in the direction of the herd, with the animal following.

The Catahoula is labeled a header, but I have seen them heel and drive a herd as well as any heeling breed. They are able to determine which tactic is needed to get the animal(s) moving, and then they apply whatever pressure or technique that is required. This instinctual factor may be found in most Catahoulas. They may require some guidance in when and where to use it, but most are born with the ability to provide service.

The art of bunching a herd together and holding them in position is known as Baying. Baying is performed by barking, nipping, and circling an animal or herd to hold it in one location. This action is performed to enable a handler to approach without scattering the herd, and drive them in a specific direction with the dogs following behind. The dogs will follow, but not interfere with the herd unless directed by the handler. Herding one hundred head of cattle with three dogs and one rider is not an unusual task.

Hunting, tracking, search and rescue, and recovery can be combined into one category. Each of these is a means of using the dog's ability to isolate a specific scent, known as scent discrimination, and follow it to the source. To many people this seems to be an amazing task, but, it is an inherited trait in most working, hunting, and herding dogs. Once the dog understands what you want him to locate, he will oblige you.

The Catahoula is quiet on the trail, which provides hunters with the ability to acquire their game without having the game retreat before they arrive. A barking dog may forewarn the game of their approach, giving it an opportunity to escape. Once the game is located, the Catahoula will give voice to indicate that he has located it and is holding it in position. This works extremely well when hunting wild boar, bear, mountain lion, and most large game. Catahoulas may be taught to give voice, or bark, while on the trail, but it is not common for them to do so.

One of the characteristics of the Catahoula is its ability to locate its prey by air scenting. If the scent can be detected in the air or on the wind, they will track to the location where it lies, then return to the handler. The handler will then follow them back to the origin of the scent. Hunters have successfully used this technique to locate game that has been wounded. This is often referred to as blood trailing; however, there does not have to be the presence of blood for it to be successful. The scent of the animal is all that is required. This same method of trailing is used in search and rescue, and body recovery. The dog is presented with a specific scent, given a command to begin working, and off he goes to locate the source. Dogs performing body recovery are referred to as Cadaver Dogs. The dog is taught to locate the source of a deceased person, whether buried under rubble, earth, or submerged in water. Deceased victims exude a specific odor and the dogs are taught to isolate the location of the source.

There was a time when I would profess that a Catahoula was not much of a retriever. That misconception has been put to rest. There are bird hunters who use their Catahoulas to retrieve ducks and quail. This is not my area of expertise, but seeing them perform has made me a believer.

In spite of its natural air-scenting abilities, the Catahoula can be taught to put its nose to the ground to perform specific scent identification. Arson, narcotics, and explosives detection are very similar in their operational procedure. Although the dog does not have to travel over long distances to locate the source, he is taught to identify a specific scent, isolate the source, and give an alert to its location. The most common type of alert is called the passive alert, which has the dog assume a sitting position at the location of the source. Some arson and narcotics dogs are taught the active alert, which is to alert by scratching at the location of the source. Explosives detection dogs are never taught an active alert. Scratching at explosives could result in fatal consequences. They simply locate the source and sit quietly until the handler releases them.

Remo demonstrates his ability to retrieve a quail. The author once believed that Catahoulas did not make good retrievers.

Service assistance dogs are used to help individuals who are unable to perform day-to-day tasks. Most training agencies do not use the Catahoula due to its defensive nature to protect its owner. In their opinions, this is not a desirable trait. Although there are not many used by service agencies, Catahoulas are being used by private owners who have received help in training their Catahoula to assist them. For example, Catahoulas are taught to pick up items that have been dropped and are out of the reach of persons who are incapable of picking them up on their own. Their ability to perform assistance tasks improve with each passing day.

Many people have commented on the Catahoulas' webbed feet. The fact is that most dogs have webbed feet, but the Catahoulas' webs extend almost to the first joint on the toes, very similar to those of a duck. This enables them to walk and run with ease across difficult terrains, such as swamps and sand.

Natural bob-tailed Catahoulas date back before they were ever registered. When this phenomenon occurred is anybody's guess. I know that they were in existence and used in north Louisiana as far back as the early 1850s. Hand-written records and conversations with farmers' families have provided proof of their presence and use. The majority of breeders do not like the bob-tail for reasons of their own, but the absence of a tail is not detrimental to the function of the breed.

The desired size and weight of a Catahoula is between 65 and 75 pounds for males, and between 55 and 65 pounds for females. The average height of a male is 22 to 26 inches, with females measuring between 20 and 24 inches at the withers. The ideal size and weight is the average of the ranges. There are some Catahoulas that measure as tall as 28 inches and weigh as much as 110 pounds. These are genetic anomalies displaying the Wright line of dogs.

This breed is more at home on a farm working livestock or in the woods hunting, but can be a fine house pet if it receives enough exercise. Exercise is the key ingredient in keeping a Catahoula as a house pet. You must be prepared to exercise this dog for about one hour each day, rain or shine. Providing an energy outlet can involve such things as tracking and agility, or accompanying you while jogging, biking, horseback riding, or any activity that allows the release of their energy. They have been known to remove the woodwork from a home when they become bored or anxious, so if you are keeping them indoors, be sure they are exercised.

In the introduction, I made reference to working dogs. A working dog is one that performs a task for which it is intended. Most ranchers and hunters will scoff at a dog that does not perform herding or hunting feats. This is a misinterpretation of the word "work." Any dog that performs a specific function for the benefit of humans is considered a working dog. For example, a ranch hand is required to gather, or round up, a herd of cattle. He will choose the dog that will best suit his needs and go about his business. In the same vein, the search and recovery unit will choose the dog that best suits their needs. To say that the SAR dog is not a working dog is a misnomer. If you were to ask a rancher, "If your child were lost out in the wilderness, which dog would you want looking for him, a stock dog or a search dog?" you can bet it will not be his best herding dog. Whenever speaking of working dogs, it is best to clarify what type of work, or working style, you desire.

Assertive is the best way to describe a Catahoula's attitude. They are not normally aggressive, but will stand their ground when challenged. This is a dog that wants to be in charge and will test every fiber of your being. In multiple dog households, the Catahoula is generally the alpha dog, and obedience training is advised for all Catahoula owners.

Independent, wary of strangers, protective of what and whom he thinks he owns, steadfast, loyal, hardworking, efficient, affectionate, and gentle with its family, all describe the Catahoula. This is a strong breed that requires a firm hand of control—one that is not brutal, but firm and fair. This is a breed that will do its best to please you, regardless of your use. This is a Dog of Distinction.

Conformation Standard

THE conformation standard, commonly referred to as the breed standard, is the measure by which we gauge the acceptable appearance and structure of the Catahoula. The original breed standard was designed by breeders and owners who worked their dogs in the field and hunted wild game with them. It was in their opinion the guide to be followed in producing the perfect dog. Unfortunately, the perfect dog does not exist. Many have come close, but there is always a fault or flaw that will prevent it from being perfect. Knowing that the perfect dog cannot be produced should not be your guide to the production of inferior dogs.

The term "conformation" tends to confuse some people into believing that this is a fancy term for a show dog. It is not. Let me explain what conformation is and why it is important.

Conformation is the term used to encompass the total composition of the dog. It is a means of examining a dog without the aid of elaborate X-ray equipment. By following the standard, you may determine the proper skull shape, ear set, eye set and formation, bite (the position of the teeth set in the jaw, and those that are missing), nose length and breadth, depth and breadth of chest, height (as measured from the withers, or top of shoulder, to forefoot), weight, proper set of front legs, topline (the backbone from shoulder to rump), tail set and carriage, rear leg set and angulation, and tuck (the area between rear leg and stomach). In addition to visibly and physically examining the dog, there is the dog's movement, or the manner in which the dog places his feet while walking and referred to as his gait. In a forward movement, the foreleg should fall just at the end of the dog's nose, and the rear leg should fall in the same spot that the forefoot previously occupied. Independent movement of the legs is also a requirement that is often overlooked.

Pacing is when both front and rear legs move together in the same direction. Both the left rear and left front will move forward and backward simultaneously, and then will repeat on the right side. This movement will hamper the dog in performing efficiently.

This standard has nothing to do with the manner in which the dog works, but it has everything to do with the dog's efficiency to do the job. That is why conformation is so important. Every effort should be made to produce the perfect specimen, for your effort will be rewarded with knowledge of their structure and ability, and the production of a quality line of dogs that others will be eager to own.

The Catahoula standard is written as a guide to breeding for the perfect specimen, but there is the issue of interpretation. It is known that when several people read the same written text, several versions of that text will be produced. Keeping this in mind, you should seek out reputable breeders who are using the same registry standard that you have chosen. Through the years, I have found that most experienced Catahoula breeders are willing to share their ideas and experiences, and offer assistance to new breeders. Ask for their input, view their dogs and accomplishments, and discuss the various opinions that you encounter. Become a computer, if you will, by sorting through all of the data collected. Extract what is important, place it in a file where it will not be lost, and delete the rest.

Although most Catahoula standards are similar in their description of the breed, there remain some variances within each registry. In order to avoid any conflicts in a breeding program, it is advisable that the breed standard for each chosen registry be reviewed and understood.

The breeder, more so than the exhibitor, should be aware of the variations in breed standards among the different registries. What may appear as a minor infraction, or fault, could result in your changing your entire line of breeding. Many years of dedicated breeding have been vested with this breed, and any new breeder should beware of adopting a registry that is not true to the working dog. Some registries will adopt a breed, change the standard to present what they think "looks good," and lose sight of the ability and function of a true Catahoula. Too many working breeds have been ruined by organizations that modify the standards for the purpose of appearance. The United Kennel Club standard was adopted from the original standards developed by the National Association of Louisiana Catahoulas, the official Louisiana registry. Any changes made to the UKC breed standard are voted on by the breed's parent club, which has authority over the standard. Changes are made when genetic discoveries are proven and have a direct bearing on the reproduction of the breed, and not merely for aesthetic value. The UKC is a registry that recognizes a true working dog, and does not discount points in the conformation ring for dogs whose scars were earned through their labor.

The following Catahoula standard is the model used by the United Kennel Club, and it is reprinted here with their permission.

LOUISIANA CATAHOULA LEOPARD DOG
Herding Dog Group
Official U.K.C. Breed Standard
©Copyright 1994, United Kennel Club, Inc.
Revised January 1, 2008

HISTORY
The origins of the Louisiana Catahoula Leopard Dog are unknown but it is believed to be descended from crosses between Native American dogs, Red Wolves (some of whom lived as pariahs on the outskirts of Indian villages), and the dogs brought to the New World by Spanish conquistadors, probably mastiff-types and sight hounds. Some experts believe Beaucerons were added to the mix when the area was settled by the French. White settlers in Louisiana found the Native Americans using these unusual-looking dogs to hunt a variety of wild game, including deer, bobcat, wild hog, and bear. The new arrivals soon came to appreciate this versatile breed that was equally capable of scenting, trailing and treeing game, or baying and herding feral hogs and cattle.

There are many stories regarding the origin of the breed's exotic name: Catahoula. The most likely is that it is a corruption of the Indian word that meant "Choctaw," the name of a local tribe.

The only thing certain is that the Louisiana Catahoula Leopard Dog is an all-American, multi-purpose working dog. On July 9, 1979, the governor of Louisiana signed a bill making this breed the official State Dog of Louisiana.

The Louisiana Catahoula Leopard Dog was recognized by the United Kennel Club on January 1, 1995.

GENERAL APPEARANCE

The Louisiana Catahoula Leopard Dog is a medium to medium-large, short-coated dog, with a broad head, small-to-medium drop ears, and an undocked tail set on as a natural extension of the topline. The Catahoula is well muscled and powerful, but not bulky, giving the impression of agility and endurance. The Catahoula is a moderate breed and should not resemble either a sight hound or a bulldog in appearance. The body is just slightly longer than tall and the distance from the elbow to the ground should equal 50-60 percent of the dog's height from the withers to the ground. Because of the breed's name, many people assume that all Catahoulas have the so-called "leopard" markings and blue eyes. In fact, the breed is noted for its many and unusual coat colors and patterns, as well as varied eye color. The Catahoula should be evaluated as a multi-purpose working dog, and exaggerations or faults should be penalized in proportion to how much they interfere with the dog's ability to work.

CHARACTERISTICS

Catahoula temperament ranges from serious and business-like when working to clownish at home, with varying levels of energy. It is not uncommon for Catahoulas to be aloof with strangers, which often results in a lack of animation when showing and may cause some to draw away from judges when being examined. Catahoulas should never be excessively aggressive or shy. They can be independent, protective and territorial so they require firm guidance and a clear understanding of their place in the family unit. Catahoulas are affectionate, gentle and loyal family companions.

HEAD

The head is powerfully built without appearing exaggerated. Viewed from the side, the length of skull and muzzle are approximately equal in length, and joined by a well-defined stop of moderate length. The planes of the topskull and the bridge of the muzzle are roughly parallel to one another. There may be a slight median furrow between the eyes and running back to the occipital bone. Gender differences should be apparent in the characteristics of the head.

SKULL - The skull is broad and flat. The cheeks are well developed.
Fault: Excessively broad skull; narrow skull.
MUZZLE - The muzzle is strong and deep. Viewed from above, the muzzle is moderately wide and tapering toward the nose. Lips may be tight or slightly pendulous with pigment of any color or combination of colors.
Faults: Snipey muzzle.
TEETH - The Louisiana Catahoula Leopard Dog has a complete set of evenly spaced, white teeth. A scissors bite is preferred, but a level bite is acceptable. Full dentition is greatly desired, but dogs are not to be penalized for worn or broken teeth.
Serious Faults: Overshot or undershot bite.
NOSE - Nose pigment may be any color or combination of colors.
EYES - Eyes are set moderately well apart, medium in size, somewhat rounded in appearance, and are set well into the skull. Eyes may be any color or combination of colors without preference. Eye rims are tight and may be any color or combination of colors.
Serious Faults: Malformed pupils; pupils not centered; sagging eyelids making haw visible; functional abnormality of eyelids or eyelashes.
EARS - Ears are drop, short to medium in length, moderate in size, and proportionally wide at the base, gradually tapering to the slightly rounded tip. They should fold over and be generally triangular in shape. The top of the ear fold is level or just slightly below the top line of the skull. When the dog is at attention, the inner edge of the ear lies close to the cheek. Laid-back ears are acceptable but not preferred.
Faults: Any ear type other than described above.
Disqualification: Cropped ears.

NECK
The neck is muscular and of good length, without being overdone. The circumference of the neck widens from the nape to where the neck blends smoothly into the shoulders.
Faults: Neck too short and thick or too thin and weak; excess skin forming dewlap.

FOREQUARTERS
The shoulders are strong and smoothly muscled. The shoulder blades are long, wide, flat and well laid back. The upper arm is roughly equal in length to the shoulder blade and joins it at an angle sufficient to ensure that the foot falls under the withers. The elbows are close to the body and do not turn out.
FORELEGS - The forelegs are straight, and of medium bone, indicating strength without excessive thickness. Pasterns are strong, short, and slightly sloping. The length of the forelegs should roughly

equal 50-60% of the dog's height at the withers. A dog with legs shorter than the ideal is to be more heavily penalized than a dog with longer legs.

Faults: Forequarters significantly heavier than hindquarters; bone too heavy or too fine; straight shoulders; out at elbows; weak pasterns.

BODY

A properly proportioned Louisiana Catahoula Leopard Dog is slightly longer than tall. The topline inclines very slightly downward from well-developed withers to a level back. The back is broad and well muscled with a short, strong, slightly arched loin. A slightly longer loin is acceptable in females. The ribs extend well back and are well sprung out from the spine. The chest is deep, reaching at least to the elbows, and moderately broad. When viewed from the side, the forechest extends in a shallow oval shape in front of the forelegs. Tuck-up is apparent, but not exaggerated. Croup is medium to long and slightly sloping. A slightly elevated rear resulting from slightly straighter rear angulation should not be penalized too severely.

Faults: Chest too broad, too narrow or too shallow; soft topline; exaggerated or absent tuck-up; loin too long.

HINDQUARTERS

Hindquarters are strong and smoothly muscled. Width and angulation of hindquarters are in balance with the forequarters.

HIND LEGS - The stifles are well bent and the hocks are well let down. When the dog is standing, the short, strong rear pasterns are perpendicular to the ground and, viewed from the rear, parallel to one another.

Faults: Thin, weak hindquarters; cow-hocked; open-hocked.

FEET

Good feet are essential for a working dog. Feet are well knit and oval in shape. Toes are long, webbed, and well arched. Pads are thick and hard. Nails are strong. Dewclaws may be removed.

Fault: Cat foot.

TAIL

The tail is a natural extension of the topline. It is thicker at the base, and tapers to the tip. Natural bob tails are permitted, but not preferred. The natural bob tail, regardless of length, will taper in width from base to tip. A full length tail may be carried upright with the tip curving forward when the dog is moving or alert. When the dog is relaxed, the tail hangs naturally, reaching to the hock joint. Catahoulas should be allowed to carry their tails naturally when being shown. Exhibitors should not hold tails upright.

Faults: Ring tail; docked tail.

Disqualification: Complete absence of a tail (no external coccygeal vertebrae evident).

COAT

The Catahoula has a single coat, short to medium in length, that lies flat and close to the body. Texture ranges from smooth to coarse, without preference.

Disqualifications: Long coat; fuzzy coat that obscures the outline of the dog.

COLOR

Catahoulas come in an endless variety of coat colors and patterns. All color combinations and patterns can have color points or trim, which may be located on the chest, cheeks, above the eyes, on the legs, underbody or under the tail. The Leopard pattern has a base color with contrasting spots of one or more other colors. Solids have a single coat color. Brindles may have a light or dark base coat color with contrasting stripes. The Patchwork pattern may or may not have one predominant solid color with one or more different size patches of different colors and shades placed randomly on the body. In dogs of equal quality, rich, deep colors are preferable to the lighter colors. However, in evaluating the Catahoula as a true, multi-purpose working dog, coat color is not a primary consideration. No coat color or pattern is preferred.

Serious Fault: 70 percent or more white.

Disqualifications: 90 percent or more white coat color; solid white head; albinism.

HEIGHT AND WEIGHT

Ideal height at maturity for males is 24 inches, and for females, 22 inches, with a variation of two inches either way acceptable. Weight may range from 50 to 95 pounds, in proportion to the dog's height. The Louisiana Catahoula Leopard Dog must be both powerful and agile, so actual weight and height are less important than the correct proportion of weight to height. Catahoulas should always be presented in hard, working condition. Any deviation from the ideal must be judged by the extent of the deviation, and the effect it has on the dog's ability to work.

GAIT

When trotting, the gait is smooth, fluid and effortless, showing good but not exaggerated reach in front and powerful drive behind. The topline remains level with only a slight flexing to indicate suppleness. Viewed from any position, legs turn neither in nor out, nor do feet cross or interfere with each other. As speed increases, feet tend to converge toward center line of balance. Poor movement should be penalized to the degree to which it reduces the Catahoula's ability to perform the tasks it was bred to do.

DISQUALIFICATIONS

Unilateral or bilateral cryptorchid. Viciousness or extreme shyness. Unilateral or bilateral deafness. Cropped ears. Long coat. Fuzzy coat that obscures the outline of the dog. 90 percent or more white coat color. Solid white head. Albinism. Complete absence of a tail (no external coccygeal vertebrae evident).

United Kennel Club Inc.
100 E. Kilgore Rd.
Kalamazoo, MI 49002-5584

Genetically Speaking

THE well-informed breeder is always concerned about health, disease, and pests, but the main focus of attention is on behavior and the control of inherited genetic anomalies. In the Catahoula, there are heritable genes that can create serious problems with health and behavior, especially if the breeder is unaware of them or does not make an attempt to apply whatever controls are possible.

The Catahoula, although still considered a rare breed, has been in existence long enough that most behavior and health issues should have been addressed and/or resolved. The requirements for elimination of genetic health problems are simple; the input of numerous, dedicated breeders, and scientific studies. Unfortunately, most breeders remain active within a given breed for about five years and then they switch breeds or abandon breeding all together. Many people become breeders with the mindset that breeding dogs is profitable and simple, only to learn that a good year is making enough to pay off their feed bill at the end of that year. Due to the lack of dedicated breeders and grants to fund the projects needed, there are genetic anomalies that remain a mystery.

The major issues facing Catahoula breeders are deafness, blindness, sterility, hip dysplasia, and a small gene pool. The merle gene and the probable presence of the piebald gene are the main ingredients for the bulk of deafness issues facing Catahoula breeders.

Time and again, you will hear breeders remark on how you should know and understand the genetic composition and how it influences the outcome of a litter. That sounds like a simple task, but in most cases the reader, in order to understand what they have read, is required to have a medical reference dictionary at their disposal. The following glossary contains the more common terms you will encounter in your quest to breeding better Catahoulas.

Allele – One of a pair or series of genes occupying a specific position on a chromosome.

Artificial insemination – A means of placing sperm in the female's reproductive tract.

Autosomal – Any nonsexual chromosome.

Bilateral – Involving two sides.

Birth Defect – Abnormality occurring at birth (structural, functional, or metabolic).

Blindness – Lacking the sense of sight.

Carrier – Possessing one of the alleles required to produce a specific disease.

Chromosome – Any of the threadlike bodies carrying the genes.

Deafness – Lacking the sense of hearing.

Dominant – One of a pair of alleles that masks the other.

Dysplasia – Genetic disorder affecting the hip and elbow joints.

Eumelanin – Black, its derivatives, or brown coloration.

Gene – The basic unit of heredity.

Gene Pool – The total number of genes possessed by a specific breed.

Genotype – The genetic makeup of organisms not displayed.

Heterozygous – Having a dissimilar pair of genes.

Homozygous – Having an identical pair of genes.

In-Breeding – Individuals immediately related (father/daughter, mother/son, brother/sister).

Inheritance – Genetic characteristic transmitted from parent to offspring.

Line Breeding – Selective in-breeding of individuals related within the first or second ancestry (grandparent/grandchild, half-brother/half-sister, uncle/niece, aunt/nephew, and cousins).

Locus – The location of a gene on a chromosome.
Malformation – Structural defect inherited during fetal development.
Melanin – A pigment or color in skin and hair.
Merle – A gene responsible for diluting color which creates a mixture or blotching of color or combination of colors. Double Merle is an added amount of merle, often referred to as excessive white.
Mutation – A permanent DNA structural alteration.
Outcross – Two individuals with no relationship to each other in any generation.
Phenotype – The outward appearance.
Piebald – Having patches of black and white, sometimes referred to as "parti-colored" or displaying no coloration on the entire face.
Polygenic – One of a group of genes determining the degree of a characteristic.
Recessive – One of a pair of alleles that is masked by the other.
Sterility – Lacking the ability to reproduce.
Surgical Insemination – Surgically implanting semen into the female's ovaries.
Syndrome – A pattern of abnormalities or symptoms.
Trait – A genetically determined characteristic.
Unilateral – Involving one side.

The Catahoula is an extremely healthy dog with very few genetic anomalies. Some disorders may raise concerns for Catahoula breeders, but most problems and concerns can be reduced through careful screening of the selected pair prior to breeding. Little has been done in the way of research on the genetic disorders that affect the Catahoula. In most projects conducted in the past, where the Catahoula was a part of a research study, the results of those studies were generally inconclusive because of the small numbers of specimens being tested. Of late, with the Catahoula becoming more popular, research is being performed in the areas of deafness and merle, and their effects on the Catahoula. Acquiring funding for various projects is the hardest obstacle to overcome.

As a breeder and in an effort to reduce or eliminate the occurrences of genetic disorders in the Catahoula, it is your responsibility to study the results of research performed on other breeds that may also affect the Catahoula. Most of the disorders affecting the Catahoula are classified as polygenic. This means that each of the breeding pair carries one allele for the disorder which, when combined, is passed on to the offspring, where it becomes more apparent.

HEARING
The Catahoula is known to produce offspring with either bilateral or unilateral deafness. It is believed that the merle gene is the cause of this problem, but there are factors that lend credence to the presence of the piebald gene being the cause.

SKELETAL
Panosteitis – The dog develops a limp or lameness that shifts from one leg to another. A fever may be present, and the dog may also show signs of anorexia and/or lethargy. It has been recommended that foods generating rapid bone growth not be used, as this could be a contributing factor. There is no definitive proof that this is true. Medications to ease the discomfort are generally prescribed and the dog will outgrow it.
Jaw - Abnormal growth of the lower jaw, resulting in an overbite or underbite.
Dysplasia - Both the hip and elbow joints can be affected, causing pain and lameness. For more details, see the chapter "Hips," starting on p. 51.
Eyes—Blindness and malformed pupils which are generally recognized by:
1. A pupil that is fixed and will not dilate, making it harder to see at night;
2. A pupil that appears to be spread out, or is off center;
3. A pupil that is not formed to a circular pattern.

DISEASE
Diabetes - The accumulation of sugar in the blood due to the inefficient use of insulin. Signs are excessive water consumption, frequent urination, and strong-smelling urine.
Hypothyroidism - Signs are dry, flaky skin, excessive weight gain, lethargy, and hair loss. It is also counterproductive to reproduction, causing

small litters or no litters after being bred. Blood tests including T3 and T4 screening will aid in the determination of its presence.

Unfortunately, we may never know the cure for these disorders due to the lack of funding for the research. The United States Department of Agriculture, which licenses and regulates most commercial breeding kennels and establishes the laws concerning canines, does not allocate any money or grants in the field of canine genetic research. Without grant money or donations to support a specific project, we may never establish the research required to determine a cure for these diseases. Knowing the causes of these disorders would enable us to curtail them within our breed as well as many others.

Many of the disorders encountered when breeding Catahoulas are considered polygenic. Polygenic pertains to two or more genes that contribute equally to an undesired effect and display no dominance. Each allele adds to the effect equally. The effect is completely dependent on the genes and not the outside environment.

Coat

THE Catahoula is most recognizable by its spotted, splotchy, or mottled coat color. The mottled coat in a Catahoula is referred to as a leopard coat, but is scientifically known as merle. Leopard colors may be black, gray, blue, red, and liver. Patched coats may be any combination of small patches of color on a white background. Solid colors may be black, red, chocolate, or yellow. Brindle is an acceptable color and although listed as a solid, it is not. Brindle consists of vertical stripes of tan appearing on a black background. Trim colors appearing on the face and legs may be tan, buff, red, black, white, or brindle.

The merle gene, being a dilutant, basically washes out the solid color that would have normally appeared. It does not dilute evenly, but presents variations or spotting within the solid colors. This is what creates the spotting of blue and gray on what otherwise would have been a black dog. The same effects may be seen on brown-colored dogs, which are referred to as red leopards. Blue leopards are black dogs with much more merle displayed. Patchwork dogs are white with large patches of varied colors.

Some tweed patterns have been incorrectly identified as patchworks. Tweed is a derivative of merle and displays the patches in a larger and more distinct pattern. Dark and light patches appear throughout, but are separated by the white base coat.

Previous references expressed by Catahoula breeders concerning merle-to-merle breeding largely have been based on the results of studies of the dappled Dachshund and the Australian Shepherd. The merle gene in the Catahoula is the same gene as in other breeds; however, research indicates that the effects of the merle gene in the Catahoula differ from that of the Australian Shepherd. In a study comparing the two breeds, there appears to be another modifier affecting the merle gene in the Catahoula that is not present in the Australian Shepherd. Because of this modifier, breeding merle to merle, or double merles, in the Catahoula is not dangerous, as was once believed.

Another myth that has been perpetuated is that when breeding a double merle, a black puppy cannot be produced. Black puppies have always been identified aesthetically as non-merle. However, DNA testing has now proven that puppies identified phenotypically as being black, or non-merle, may actually be cryptic, or ghost, merle. A cryptic merle appears to be a solid color, but when DNA testing is performed, it may indicate that the dog is genotypically a single merle. There are more cryptic merles that are being identified and bred as non-merle than was originally estimated. DNA testing of solid-colored dogs is the only sure answer. In the figure below, the puppy number 4, although black in appearance, proved to be a single merle by use of DNA testing.

A recent Texas A&M University study on the effects of the merle gene in Australian Shepherds also included a selection of Catahoulas. Although no definitive answer could be given, there was evidence to suggest that the

Cryptic merle

merle gene affects the Catahoula differently than the Australian Shepherd. Leigh Anne Clark, PhD, explains: "Fifteen of the double merles tested were Catahoula Leopard Dogs and of these, only four were deaf. Although the sample size is small, this study suggests that only about 26% of double merle Catahoula Leopard Dogs are deaf, while roughly 85% of double merles from other breeds tested (Australian Shepherd, Collie, and Shetland Sheepdog) are deaf. This finding is not entirely surprising, because double merle Catahoula Leopard Dogs exhibit larger amounts of pigmentation than do other breeds."

In similar research performed at Louisiana State University, a comparison of merle genes in the Catahoula and other merle canines was studied. This showed that the action of the merle gene on hearing differed in the Catahoula from the other breeds within the group. George M. Strain, PhD, states: "It seems clear that the risk for deafness in single merles is no greater than that in some piebald breeds such as the Dalmatian, and even in double merles, the risk is not the disaster portrayed in some breed publications."

The merle gene is one that requires a great deal of study to understand. This is an unpredictable and complicated gene. What you need to know as a breeder is that you are working with three different genotypes—single merle (Mm); double merle (MM); and non-merle (mm). For many years, breeders believed that double merle Catahoulas were taboo and should not be bred. It was believed that dogs predominantly white in color were double merle, would produce deafness, and should not be bred; however, many colored Catahoulas may also be double merle and are not deaf. For example, both puppies 1 and 3 in the picture at left are double merle, while puppies 2 and 4 are single merle.

Strain goes on to say: "In the two breeds with the greatest number of subjects, the Catahoula and Australian Shepherd, only 5.9% of Catahoulas were affected (3/54), while 9.4% of Australian Shepherds were affected (3/32). Of the double merles, only 3 of 29 Catahoulas were affected (10.3%), while 2 of 3 Australian Shepherds were affected (66.7%)."

So, as shown in these studies, double merles displaying a majority of white appear to be more susceptible to deafness, blindness, and sterility. Double merles that are free of these traits, however, should not necessarily be excluded from any breeding program. As with any dog you intend to breed, you must weigh all of its traits and ensure the use of a mate that will offset the negative ones prior to introduction to your breeding program. In other words, always breed up.

There is evidence that the piebald gene is the cause of deafness in other breeds and is widely assumed to be present in the Catahoula, although it has never been identified in them. As of this writing, there are no definitive tests that may be performed to positively identify this gene in Catahoulas and whether it contributes to deafness in the breed. There is uncertainty as to whether the merle gene or the piebald gene is the cause of the problem, or if it is a combination of the two.

The piebald gene has been identified and classified into three different recessive alleles: Irish spotting, piebald, and extreme piebald. The dominant allele produces color. Irish spotting is defined as having white confined to the neck, feet, underbody, and tail tip, with a blaze on the face of a colored dog. Piebald displays itself in many ways, but generally produces a dog that is more than 50% white or has large patches of color on a white body. This is often referred to as a patchwork in Catahoulas. Extreme piebald is displayed as a nearly all-white body with a colored head and a few spots on the body and near the tail, such as seen in the Toy Fox Terrier. Many Catahoula breeders advocate breeding for Irish spotting, touting it to be the safest of the three, and will encourage others to breed for this trait.

Although many breeders believe double merle to be the cause of the deafness problem, I believe the problem to be piebald. My belief is based on production of four litters from two sets of double merle parents. Of the four litters produced, only one puppy, which was predominantly white, was deaf. If double merle breeding in the Catahoula were as disastrous as that of the Australian Shepherd, there should have been four litters of totally deaf puppies.

In spite of the two studies described here and the valuable information gleaned from them, it remains a constant that two light-colored dogs should not be bred together. When choosing a breeding pair, it is best to mate light color to dark color; medium color to medium or dark color; and dark color to dark color.

When choosing dark-colored dogs, phenotype alone may not be the answer. DNA testing is required to determine whether a dark dog is a single merle or a non-merle. Phenotype is a guide, but not the answer.

The same is true for dogs that have been visually identified as single merle, but proved to be double merle when tested (see puppies 1 and 3 on page 36). Through DNA testing, the guesswork formerly involved with the reproduction of merle Catahoulas has been removed. It is not the complete answer, but it is a giant step forward in helping to reduce some of the guesswork facing breeders today.

Colors aside, the coat of a Catahoula is short, with some so short that it appears as if the hair had been painted on the dog. This is not to say that there are some Catahoulas with longer hair. The hair can be wooly, sometimes referred to as fuzzy, and have a length the same as that of a German Shepherd. It is widely believed that this type of coat is the appearance of the wolf or ancient Wool Dogs. Of the two, the shorter hair is preferred.

Eyes

THE Catahoulas' eye color can be as alluring as its coat color. Eye color is also affected by the merle gene. The iris, or colored portion of the eye, may be colored brown, amber (a lighter shade of brown), green, or blue. Blue eyes are commonly referred to as glass eyes. Glass eyes have varying hues, including a hue that appears almost white. The lighter glass eyes, or almost white eyes, are commonly referred to as cotton eyes. Cotton eyes are still labeled as glass because the eye color is not actually white, but the lightest shade of blue.

Heterochromia iridis is the scientific name for the presence of two opposite-colored eyes or the presence of two colors within one eye. This is more predominantly seen in dogs with glass eyes, where the iris will contain a second color. Eyes containing two or more colors are often referred to as cracked eyes. In the Catahoula, any color or combination of colors is possible and accepted.

Not only does the merle gene affect the color of the eye, but it is believed to be the cause of blindness. It has not been scientifically proven that the merle gene is the cause of blindness; however, the majority of blindness occurs within white and white-faced puppies. This adds to the belief that the cause of blindness may result from the presence of the piebald gene. Until further research is performed to determine the presence of the piebald gene in the Catahoula, we have to assume that the merle gene is the culprit. In order to determine blindness, you must wait until a suspect puppy is approximately four weeks of age, and then observe its actions when placed in locations that are unfamiliar to it. If it cannot navigate in the unfamiliar areas, it should undergo a full eye examination by a veterinarian or a certified veterinary ophthalmologist.

The pupil, which is the black portion of the eye, should be centered within the iris and respond to changes in light by dilating (widening) and constricting (narrowing). The widening and narrowing of the pupil allows only the proper amount of light to enter the eye, preventing it from becoming damaged. To determine if a pupil is responding properly, the swinging flashlight method may be used. As a small penlight-type flashlight is passed back and forth in front of the eye, the pupil should respond by closing, becoming smaller, when the light is directly in the eye, and opening, becoming larger, when it is removed.

Malformations and diseases of the eye can be of a heritable nature and are important factors when breeding Catahoulas. Although there are many diseases that can be associated with the eye, I have listed those most often confronting the Catahoula breeder.

Corectopia is the clinical term for an eccentric pupil, or one that is not centered within the iris. Eccentric pupils are most often discovered when the eyes are initially examined by the breeder or veterinarian. Caution should be taken with eyes containing spots, flakes, or flecks of color dispersed within the iris and near the pupil. These spots of color can give the appearance of an eccentric pupil, but having the eye more closely examined by a veterinarian or veterinary ophthalmologist may reveal a separation between the pupil and the colored portion.

Microphthalmia is an abnormally small eye and can affect either or both eyes.

Microcornea is an abnormally small cornea, developed when the outer convex fibrous coat covering the iris and pupil are abnormally thin or flat.

Microcoria is a congenital contraction, or smallness, of the pupil caused by the absence or lack of development of the muscles that dilate the pupils.

Cataract is a cloudiness or white film covering the eye known as lens opacity.

Coloboma is the absence of ocular tissue caused by failure of fetal fissure closure.

If any of these should occur within your breeding, you should not breed the same two dogs to each other again. Instead, choose different partners for each of them and monitor the litters. Should the disease present itself again in a subsequent breeding, the problematic dog(s) should be removed from the breeding program, and spayed or neutered to prevent any future defective litters.

The Canine Eye Registration Foundation (CERF) is an organization that certifies and registers dogs that are free of heritable eye disease. CERF works closely with the American College of Veterinary Ophthalmologists (ACVO), which certifies veterinarians in the specialized field of ophthalmology. A certified veterinary ophthalmologist will provide the actual eye examination and then complete the CERF application, indicating their findings. If the dog is found to be free of disease, the card may be sent to CERF along with the required fee. CERF will assign your dog a unique registration number, indicating that the dog is free of heritable eye disease.

Deafness

DEAFNESS may be acquired or congenital. Acquired deafness may be caused by trauma, infection, drug reaction, environmental noises, and, more commonly, old age. Acquired deafness may affect one or both ears, and may cause partial or complete deafness. This type of deafness cannot be inherited or passed on to offspring.

Congenital deafness is frequently inherited and may be unilateral or bilateral. Unilateral affects one ear, while bilateral affects both ears. Congenital deafness is generally detectable at about three weeks of age. When solid food feeding is initiated, deaf puppies may be seen sleeping through mealtimes or being unresponsive to calling and loud noises. Unfortunately, some deaf puppies are overlooked, because the deaf puppy will begin reacting to the movement of his littermates. Individual testing is the only true means of detection.

Although all puppies are born with hearing, deafness occurs soon after birth. The blood vessels associated with the cochlea begin to dry up and the hair cells used to detect sound will die, resulting in deafness in the puppy.

Testing for deafness may be accomplished by banging two pans together, jingling keys next to the dog's ears, or by making any loud noise that will attract the dog's attention. These tests may get a reaction from the dog; however, they do not prove that the dog is capable of hearing in both ears. If these tests are performed too close to the dog, he may react to the vibrations.

My preliminary test to check a suspect dog's hearing is performed with a piano tuning fork that is tuned to one kilocycle. The test is performed by tapping the fork and holding it approximately three inches from the dog's ear. Holding it any closer will allow the dog to react to the vibration of the instrument, not the sound waves. This is a preliminary test. If this test leaves any doubt to the dog's reaction, the next step is to have the dog tested via the Brainstem Auditory Evoked Response, or BAER test.

BAER testing is available at most veterinary schools and some veterinary offices. The test involves the placement of electrodes, known as scalp electrodes, just under the skin on the dog's head and ears. This procedure is painless. The opposite ends of the electrodes are connected to a sound source and computer. A series of clicks transmitted at about ten clicks per second is sent through insert earphones, while the computer detects the response through the electrodes and records the electrical activity within the cochlea and auditory pathways. The entire test requires ten to fifteen minutes to complete and a printout of the test results is made available to the owner.

Most knowledgeable Catahoula breeders will agree that deafness is their main concern in the production of offspring. For many years, breeders were convinced that the breeding of a double merle was the cause of the deafness problem and that identifying a double merle could be done strictly by aesthetic means. If a dog displayed a predominant amount of white, it was assumed to be a double merle. This theory was based on research results obtained from studies of the Australian Shepherd and Dachshund. The assumption was that because the Australian Shepherd displays the typical merle patterns also seen in the Catahoula, the merle gene must be identical. More recent research performed on the Catahoula by teams from Louisiana State University and Texas A&M indicates that double merle is not indicative of the amount of white displayed. Through DNA studies, it has been shown that dogs that are fully colored and display Irish Spotting (the more desirable white-blazed face, white collar, white feet, and a white tip on the tail) and have glass eyes are more likely to be double merles than was previously believed.

Armed with this information, a decision was made to study the breeding of known double merles. Seven DNA-proven double merle subjects were chosen. Subjects A, B, and F were males, and subjects C, D, E, and G were females.

A x C = 11 puppies – no deaf puppies
A x D = 8 puppies – no deaf puppies
B x D = 10 puppies – one deaf puppy
A x E = 10 puppies – no deaf puppies
B x D = 8 puppies – no deaf puppies
F x G = 9 puppies – one unilateral puppy
F x G = 8 puppies – no deaf puppies

These breedings resulted in the production of 62 puppies with no problems, one deaf puppy, and one unilaterally deaf puppy. Although this may be viewed as an incomplete study, it gives credibility to the fact that double merle may not always cause deafness in the Catahoula.

As was previously mentioned, the general consensus is that the amount of white coloring displayed by the breeding pair is indicative of the amount of deafness that will be produced. By reducing the amount of white displayed on the breeding pair, the amount of white displayed in their offspring will be controlled and the amount of deaf puppies in a litter limited. Holding to that theory, white has been proven to be the cause of deafness in Dalmatians and their white coloring is attributable to the piebald gene. Although the piebald gene has never been studied or proven to be present in the Catahoula, it appears that the similarities and effects caused by the piebald gene may be a contributing factor to deafness in the Catahoula. In fact, the favored color pattern, Irish Spotting, is one of the recessive alleles of the piebald gene. Is it not then possible that breeders continue to have problems with deafness due to their attempts to maintain Irish Spotting as a safe color pattern, but in reality are extending and expanding the piebald gene within the Catahoula? This is not to say that Irish Spotting should be avoided, but those dogs that are in good health, have good hearing, and display Irish Spotting should be treated the same as those dogs that display more than 70% white. They should be bred to a darker-colored mate without Irish Spotting. There is currently no basis to absolve merle as the cause of deafness, only that single and double merles are less likely to be deaf in Catahoulas than might have been predicted from past impressions of the role of merle.

Being aware of these facts concerning deafness, you may now see why it is so important to know or study the bloodlines of the breeding pair. Controlling white is important, but not to the degree that white should be eliminated completely. Some breeders want white excluded, with the exception of Irish Spotting; however, Irish Spotting may be part of the problem. Although safer than breeding a predominantly white dog, Irish Spotted dogs should still be bred with caution.

Dr. George Strain, PhD, Professor of Neuroscience at the School of Veterinary Medicine at Louisiana State University, is the foremost authority on deafness in dogs, and the leading researcher in the most recent study. In the 2003 study, "Deafness prevalence and pigmentation and gender associations in dog breeds at risk," Strain et al. discovered that

> a second pigmentation locus associated with deafness is that designated by M, often known by the name associated with the pattern of the dominant allele, merle. Homozygosity of the recessive allele (mm) produces uniform pigmentation, while the heterozygous merle (Mm) produces dappling or alternate body areas of fully pigmented coat and pale eumelanic or even white coat. Homozygous merles (MM) are usually nearly solid white, and in some breeds may be deaf, and blind with microphthalmic eyes. Dogs heterozygous for M are variable in their likelihood of deafness.

A more recent (2009) study by the same group, "Prevalence of deafness in dogs heterozygous or homozygous for the merle allele," states further that

> In the two breeds with the greatest number of subjects, the Catahoula and Australian shepherd, only 5.9% of Catahoulas were affected (3/54), while 9.4% of Australian shepherds were affected (3/32). Of the double merles, only 3 of 29 Catahoulas were affected (10.3%), while 2 of 3 Australian shepherds were affected (66.7%).
>
> It seems clear that the risk for deafness in single merles is no greater than that in some piebald breeds such as the Dalmatian, and even in double merles the risk is not the disaster portrayed in some breed publications.

The studies performed at LSU and Texas A&M indicate that the effects of the merle gene in the Catahoula differ from those of the Australian Shepherd, at least in severity. It is believed that the merle gene, although a modifier, is also being modified to some degree within the Catahoula.

DISPOSITION OF DEAF PUPPIES

The question of what to do with a deaf puppy has been the source of many debates and will probably go on long after I have left this earth.

Some will debate that since there is nothing physically wrong with the puppy, it should be allowed to live its life and simply be placed with a family that will care for it. There is no simple solution to a complex problem.

Take a look at deafness as it applies to humans. When a human is born deaf, the family's first instinct is to seek out methods that will help to educate and teach a means of communication. The common method of communication is the use of hand gestures, known as signing. We as a whole believe this to be a good thing for deaf humans, because they now have a means to communicate. This all seems very logical to us, and, unfortunately, the one thing overlooked in the deaf dog debate is logic.

Dogs do not function as logical thinkers, at least to the extent that humans do. Their sole means of existence is via instinct and learned response. Dogs must be taught the action we desire. You can tell them, but they are not going to comply until they are taught. That teaching is through repetitious training, and not by expressing a feeling or desire.

Deaf humans require special training, as do dogs. Placing a deaf dog in a home where the human is compassionate to the needs of the dog, but does not or cannot meet the animal's needs, is only opening the door for another human to be injured. Deaf dogs need special understanding, training, and attention by their owners, and not all deaf dogs are star pupils.

As mentioned above, we provide a means of teaching deaf humans to communicate, but we fall far short of accomplishment because the rest of the hearing world does not learn this form of communication. Deaf persons are resigned to communicate fluently with other deaf persons, but must convey their thoughts and wishes via the written word for most hearing persons to understand. It is the same as traveling in a foreign country and trying get directions.

A deaf dog is considerably more difficult to handle and may develop ill behaviors by being startled. Those ill behaviors generally take the form of biting. Is it worth the life of a dog to chance the injury of another human? As a result of negative behaviors and the excessive necessity to train deaf dogs, many experience a poor quality of life.

It is for these reasons that I believe that deaf dogs should be destroyed before being placed in a home. I make this point because if a deaf dog is placed in a home (because it was not recognized to be deaf), attachments rapidly form and it is no longer a simple matter to say that the dog should be put down. Unless the whole family, and not just one family member, is able to commit to the training, maintenance, and well-being of a deaf dog, that dog should never leave the kennel.

The following is an unedited email I received on November 23, 2008:

I have thought about you much this week, as it has been the most difficult week of my life. My husband and I contacted you through email about two and half years ago about our deaf Catahoula. You wrote back a very long and heartfelt email saying that we needed to put him down, that he was a ticking time bomb, and that no doubt it would be worse in the long run.

You were so right. We tried so hard with our Jake, exercising him, taking him to doggie daycare nearly every day, being more forceful at home with discipline. We just couldn't bring ourselves to give up on him when you told us that we should. And it worked, it seemed, for a while. Ultimately, we were unable to help him. His aggression against us was unpredictable and dangerous. He got worse over these two and half years, and bit several people. Luckily, amazingly, no one sued us or was horribly hurt. The last time was this week, when he bit me and it felt like he had cracked the bones in my hand. He didn't, but as always, the attack was unprovoked and without warning. He was sick, for he obviously loved me the most, and yet could hurt me in that way.

We had to put him down this weekend. We just couldn't do it any more. The guilt that we felt was unbelievable, but it was the only option.

Thank you for your honesty those years ago. Your words were truly always in the back of my mind. I wanted to make Jake realize that we were helping him, but he was mentally ill, mentally unable to change.

I hope that others never have to go through what we've gone through. Please pass my story along to anyone that you are counseling.

Sincerely,
Victoria Scheffler, Fort Worth, TX

Hips

CANINE hip dysplasia (CHD) is another concern of many breeders. CHD is an improper fitting of the femoral head (ball) into the acetabulum (hip socket), or an abnormal formation of the hip that creates a loose-fitting joint. As the dog ages, or exercises to extremes in the case of a working dog, the joint becomes inflamed or malformed, causing the development of degenerative joint disease (DJD). DJD develops as the surface of the bone wears and creates flakes that break off and become lodged within the socket, causing pain, instability, or immobility. Although this disease is not often seen at its most debilitating stage in Catahoulas, it does exist. It is believed that the musculature of the Catahoula provides greater stability to an irregular joint.

The means of determining the presence of DJD or CHD is to have a radiograph (X-ray) taken of the dog's rear legs. Currently there are two organizational methods used to make this determination: The Orthopedic Foundation for Animals (OFA), and the University of Pennsylvania, School of Veterinary Medicine utilizing the University of Pennsylvania Hip Improvement Program (PennHIP).

X-rays are only a snapshot in time and a determination as to whether or not a dog will develop CHD later in life cannot be made. In addition, it cannot be determined if a dog diagnosed with CHD will worsen, but it rarely ever improves. With that in mind, it would be advisable to have the tests performed at three different time intervals and take the average of the three tests.

The procedure required by OFA is to have a veterinarian take an X-ray of the dog's hips while the dog is held in the extended position. This is accomplished by placing the dog on his back, stretching the rear legs to their full extent, and turning the knees inward while maintaining a straight backbone. Positioning is extremely important in this procedure and care must be taken to ensure proper alignment in order to get an accurate X-ray. The slightest variation during the procedure could result in a failing score being assessed.

OFA prefers dogs to be anesthetized when undergoing the X-ray procedure; therefore dogs that are X-rayed while awake will be viewed differently than those under anesthetic. In their opinion, dogs that are awake and restrained during the procedure are never fully relaxed and are able to hide some faults.

X-rays to determine the condition of the hips may be taken at any time after six months, but in order to receive a hip certification from OFA, dogs must be a minimum of two years of age. Dogs under two years of age will receive a preliminary score, but not a certification number, and must be re-evaluated at two years of age.

The X-ray, along with the information card and fee, are sent to OFA, where two out of the 20 volunteer, board-certified radiologists are randomly chosen to view the X-ray. Each radiologist will scrutinize the X-ray independently and place it into one of the seven predetermined categories. If both radiologists agree on identical scores, a third radiologist is used in an effort to break the tie. If all three agree, the score is presented. If they do not agree, the average of the three will be the score.

The seven categories assigned by OFA are Excellent, Good, Fair, Borderline, Mild, Moderate, and Severe. Excellent, good, and fair are considered passing scores and the X-ray will be given an OFA certification number. Borderline, mild, moderate, and severe are considered failing scores and certification will be withheld. A dog that receives a failing score may submit a second X-ray for re-evaluation. It is recommended that the procedure used to acquire the second X-ray be reversed. If the X-ray was taken under anesthesia, then the second should be taken while the dog is awake, and vice versa.

The disadvantage to the OFA procedure is that the breeder must keep and maintain a dog for two years prior to knowing if the dog is a good candidate for his breeding program.

It should be noted that there have been dogs that received a passing certification by OFA only to develop hip problems later in life, while dogs that were failed by OFA never showed any clinical signs of failure.

PennHIP was developed by Dr. Gail Smith at the University of Pennsylvania School of Veterinary Medicine. The procedure used requires veterinarians that are trained and certified by PennHIP to take X-rays in three different views of the dog's hips while it is anesthetized. The first is the extended view recommended and used by OFA, and the next two are the distraction and compression views. The distraction and compression views are used to obtain measurements in the amount of joint laxity, or the space between the ball and socket. To acquire these X-rays, a special tool is used to position and apply a specific amount of pressure to the hip and rear legs. At the end of the X-ray procedure, the veterinarian will send radiographs to PennHIP for analysis.

PennHIP analyzes the X-rays, and, using the distraction view, measures the amount of hip laxity present. The Distraction Index (DI) is the numerical measurement obtained and assigned to the dog. This is not a subjective reading, but one that requires a physical measurement to achieve an accurate and reliable numeric value. The smaller the numeric value, the tighter the hips.

Hip scores using this procedure may be acquired beginning at four months of age. Reports indicate that performing the PennHIP procedure on dogs as young as four months of age provides results that are in direct correlation to those achieved when using OFA testing procedures at 24 months of age. The PennHIP procedure drastically shortens the waiting period required by OFA, thereby providing the breeder with a speedier evaluation of a dog intended for a breeding program.

A report published in the *Journal of American Veterinary Medical Association*, Vol.217, No.5, September 1, 2000, displayed a chart on the frequency of hip dysplasia based on a study of four breeds demonstrating a high percentage of HD. The four breeds used in this study were the English Setter (1091), Portuguese Water Dog (1101), Chinese Shar-Pei (1070), and

Bernese Mountain Dog (2941). The study was a culmination of dogs born between 1972 and 1993, and which were tested using OFA procedures between 23 and 36 months of age.

In the following chart, dogs that tested borderline (4) were eliminated from this study. The top group of boxes indicates Females and the far left group of boxes indicates Males, each with its individual OFA reading. Using the chart as you would a map, find the sex and OFA reading assigned to the dogs you wish to breed, and follow the columns to their intersecting point. The intersecting box contains the number of dysplastic dogs and the number of dogs tested, expressed as a fraction, and in parentheses the percentages of dysplasia that appeared in that breeding.

FEMALE / MALE	1 EXCELLENT	2 GOOD	3 FAIR	5 MILD	6 MODERATE	7 SEVERE
1 EXCELLENT	1/43 (2.3%)	33/348 (9.5%)	17/169 (10.6%)	3/22 (13.6%)	4/30 (13.3%)	0/2 (0.0%)
2 GOOD	51/413 (12.3%)	333/2554 (13.0%)	110/731 (15.0%)	40/197 (20.3%)	35/153 (22.9%)	1/5 (20.0%)
3 FAIR	12/94 (12.8%)	120/471 (16.2%)	55/286 (19.2%)	20/83 (24.1%)	12/43 (27.9%)	1/2 (50.0%)
5 MILD	2/6 (33.3%)	17/80 (21.2%)	7/14 (50.0%)	1/4 (25.0%)	3/9 (33.3%)	2/2 (100.0%)
6 MODERATE	5/15 (33.3%)	23/98 (23.5%)	13/32 (40.6%)	1/10 (10.0%)	1/9 (11.1%)	NA
7 SEVERE	NA	2/8 (25.0%)	1/6 (16.7%)	NA	0/3 (0.0%)	NA

In spite of the indications shown in the chart, AVMA reports that neither males nor females are more prolific in producing dysplasia, and that both contribute equally to this disease. The study demonstrates that dogs having OFA scores of Excellent when bred together had a 2.3% potential of producing HD in their offspring. This would indicate that the disease is polygenic, and its elimination is not likely. However, with careful breeding, a reduction in the number of occurrences can be obtained. The breeds used in this study have reduced their percentages of HD by following good programmed breeding practices.

In an effort to reduce the number of HD occurrences, breeders are using this information with increased success. The object here is not to eliminate a good dog from a breeding program because of a single problem, but to make an effort to reduce the problem, maintain the positive traits, and improve the line. Given the limited gene pool of the Catahoula, we cannot afford to discard dogs with positive traits and qualities. We do not have to rebuild the Catahoula. We have to make an effort to perfect it.

Both OFA and PennHIP advise that X-rays for hip evaluations should not be taken of a female in heat or one that is close to their heat cycle. Hormone levels are increased during estrus and have a direct bearing on the hip scores. Since it is a known fact that hormone levels have a direct bearing on a female's hip scores, what of a male to be tested? With a female, you can obviously tell when she is in heat, but, with a male, you cannot determine what his hormone level is at the time of testing. Males undergo a roller coaster of hormonal changes throughout their lives, especially when in the presence of a female in heat. Could that have an effect on hips and test results? I could not get an answer from OFA or PennHIP, other than it was an "interesting point."

In addition to genetic predisposition, environmental factors, food, and overexercising may contribute to HD. Puppies that are kept on newspaper or slippery surfaces are susceptible to the development of HD. Food that is too high in protein, vitamins, and minerals, being fed to dogs that do not receive enough exercise to use such intake, will become obese, which in turn hastens the development of HD.

Listed below are the addresses and Web site information for OFA, PennHIP, and AVMA. I encourage you to read as much information on this subject as possible, for the decisions you make about breeding will be displayed in the puppies you produce.

OFA, Orthopedic Foundation for Animals, 2300 E. Nifong Blvd., Columbia, MO 65201-3806 http://www.offa.org

PennHIP, University of Pennsylvania School of Veterinary Medicine, 3850 Spruce Street, Philadelphia, PA 19104 http://www.pennhip.org

AVMA, American Veterinary Medical Association, 1931 North Meacham Road, Suite 100, Schaumburg, IL 60173-4360 http://www.avma.org

Parasites

EVERY dog is susceptible to external and internal parasites, most of which can be detected and identified with periodic examinations. Being aware of the signs of their existence will aid you in identifying the parasite that you encounter and the process required to eliminate their presence.

The most obvious indication that external parasites are present on the dog is a persistent scratching or head shaking in an attempt to get relief, a stiff or dry coat, and loss of hair. Locating external parasites requires a close examination of the dog's coat and skin, including the neck, ears (inside and out), tail, legs, feet, leg pits, and stomach. Often a skin scraping is required to determine the problem. Once parasites have been found and identified, proper steps may be taken for their removal.

With the control and removal of any parasite, your dog will live a more comfortable and healthier life. Below are some of the solutions or treatments to rid your dog of external and internal parasites. This is only a guide. Consult your veterinarian to ensure that the correct diagnosis and proper treatments are being applied.

EXTERNAL PARASITES
FLEAS

There are four stages in the life cycle of the flea: egg, larvae, pupae, and adult. The interval from egg to adult is about three weeks. The adult female will lay approximately 40 eggs daily. The eggs, which fall off the host, will hatch in an environment with a high humidity and temperature ranges of 65 to 80 degrees.

Once the eggs hatch, the larvae will survive by feeding on the blood-rich feces left by the adult fleas. During this larval stage, tapeworm eggs are acquired. Temperatures above 95 degrees are deadly to the larvae, so they will seek shaded areas or move indoors. After molting three times, the larva will spin its cocoon and pupate. The time from hatching to pupating is approximately nine days.

Inside the cocoon, which is very sticky, the pupa turns into an adult flea and becomes practically invincible. During this stage, cocoons are found in areas that are warm and dry, such as soil, carpet, rugs, etc. The pupa will remain within its cocoon for as long as a year, until the timing is right for it to emerge. Emergence is determined by the approach of an unsuspecting host, which is detected by changes in sound, light patterns, vibrations, and the expulsion of carbon dioxide. Any of these will trigger the time for the young, unfed flea to leave the cocoon and take up residence on the host.

After locating a host, the adult flea will take a blood meal. By secreting an anticoagulant in its saliva, the flea is able to feed freely and will not readily leave its chosen host. It is imperative for the flea to remain on its host, because without a blood meal, the flea will die within a few weeks. The female begins laying eggs one day after her first blood meal and will continue to lay eggs until her death.

Continual scratching or chewing at the skin is the primary sign that fleas may be present. The anticoagulant within their saliva causes an itching sensation that must be scratched. Another sign is black specks of dirt on the dog's skin. To determine if the specks are flea droppings, blot them with a wet paper towel. If they leave a red imprint on the paper towel. they are probably flea feces, indicating the presence of fleas.

Treating fleas is not as simple as you might think. It is a twofold operation that involves ridding the dog of these pests, as well as destroying their environment. There are products available from your veterinarian that may be applied topically to your dog to alleviate the flea problem. Some of these are Advantage, Advantage Multi, Advantix, Frontline Plus, ProMeris, Vectra 3D, Comfortis, Revolution, Program, and Sentinel. These products effectively repel fleas from the dog, but will not eradicate those within the environment.

Fleas suck blood, which could lead to anemia in the dog. Not all dogs will scratch at flea bites. A flea comb will help to capture the presence of the fleas, but treatment is necessary to eliminate them. Each year, there are dogs that die due to the lack of treatment.

Keeping the dog's surrounding environment free of fleas requires spraying an insecticide. Carefully read the label and application method of any chemical that you use within the vicinity of your dog, as it could be toxic. If you use the services of a commercial exterminator, ensure that the chemical being used is safe for your dog.

Ridding the dog's environment of fleas will require treating the dog, his sleeping quarters, the yard or area in which he is allowed to exercise, and your home. Attacking the fleas at only one source will not eliminate the problem. Treating areas other than the dog must be done on a three-day rotation for nine days in order to kill the fleas that will hatch after spraying.

TICKS

There are 16 pages of the *Merck Veterinary Manual* containing information about ticks and the problems they cause. Although there are more than 1500 species of ticks, the four discussed here are of most concern to dog owners.

When not stuck in a dog and sucking its blood, the tick is at home in areas of fallen and rotted trees, where it is cool and damp. They may also be found in tall grass, lawns, bushes, and trees, where they wait for an unsuspecting host. Sensing the body temperature of its host, the tick attaches itself via direct contact with the passing animal, locates the softest area of penetration, and embeds its pincher-type mouth within the flesh, where it remains until it is full.

Ticks are most often found in the fleshy part of the neck, but may also be found in leg pits, genitals, between and under the toes, as well as on the tail and anal areas. They will normally avoid the back and sides of the dog due to the tighter and tougher skin, but in the case of infestation, may be found on almost any part of the dog, including the inner part of the ear.

The best means of removal is with the use of tweezers. Grasp the tick as close to the skin as possible. Apply a firm and steady pulling pressure until the tick relaxes its grip on the skin. It is best not to kill the tick while it is still embedded, as it will maintain its grip, and the head will become detached from the body. This will leave the head embedded in the skin, and possibly cause infection. Once the tick has been removed, it may be killed by placing it on a cloth soaked in rubbing alcohol and folding the cloth on top of the tick, or by dropping them into a receptacle containing rubbing alcohol.

In addition to being a real pest and having the ability to live between three months and a few years, they can transmit diseases to both dogs and humans. Ticks are also responsible for a condition known as tick paralysis, which occurs during their feeding process.

The most common tick is the brown tick, which can be found throughout the world and is known to transmit canine babesiosis, bovine anaplasmosis, East Coast fever, and Texas cattle fever. It can also spread tularemia and tick-borne typhus to human beings.

The dog tick exists in every state and transmits diseases such as Rocky Mountain spotted fever, encephalitis, tularemia, Colorado tick fever, and tick paralysis.

The black-legged or deer tick is responsible for diseases such as Lyme disease, encephalitis, babesiosis, ehrlichiosis, tularemia, and tick paralysis, and can be found along the east coast of the United States from Florida to Maine, westward into central Texas, Iowa, and Minnesota.

The lone star tick can be found from central Texas and Oklahoma eastward across the southern states, and along the Atlantic coast as far north as Maine, and is responsible for Rocky Mountain spotted fever, ehrlichiosis, and tularemia.

A tick's two-year life cycle consists of four stages: egg, larvae, nymph, and adult. The female lays her eggs on the ground, where they will hatch between two weeks and three months. Hatchlings are called larvae or seed ticks and are hungry, immature adults. At the larval stage, they only have six legs and must find a suitable host, usually birds or rodents, on which to feed. After several days of feeding on the blood of a host, they detach and fall to the ground, where they molt into nymphs.

Inactive during the winter months, nymphs become active in the spring, when they find new hosts on which to feed. Once again, after feeding, nymphs fall to the ground, where this time they molt into adults. As adults, generally in the fall, the fleas will find other hosts on which to feed and mate. After mating, they leave their hosts and fall to the ground once more. At this point, the male dies, while the female lives through the winter, laying eggs in the spring. The female is capable of laying up to 3000 eggs. If another host cannot be found, the female will feed on the litter of fleas until the following spring, when the process will be repeated.

To reduce any tick infestation, begin by cleaning up the property. Remove any debris in the area; keep grass cut short, especially in summer months; and clean out empty birdhouses or nests. This helps reduce the rodent population, which is a source of food, and prevent ticks from waiting in empty nests to feed on birds.

Chemical sprays are available to kill ticks and should be used when the grass is short. Spray around tree trunks up to approximately three feet high. The use of Sevin dust is also a good deterrent and usually will not harm the dog. Be sure to clean and spray the dog's sleeping quarters.

Last and certainly not least, wash the dog with a shampoo or use a dip solution that will repel ticks. There are collars and topical solutions that will provide some protection, but they must be checked, changed, or applied regularly.

EAR MITES

Ear mites, resembling microscopic ticks, are barely visible to the naked eye. They may be seen as white specks in the ear, but usually require a microscopic examination of ear wax to make the determination of their presence. Transmission is through physical contact with another animal that is infected.

Telltale signs of ear mites are the dog's continuous shaking of his head, scratching his ears, rubbing his ears against an object in an effort to scratch the itching sensation, or a dry, dark-brown or black waxy discharge in the ear. The discharge is comprised of wax, blood, mite feces, and biochemicals that are produced due to inflammation. The discharge is very similar to that of a dog with a yeast infection and can be misidentified by the owner. Before treating, it is best to have it diagnosed.

The life cycle of the mite is strange, to say the least. Mites require three weeks to go from egg to adult, living for only two months. Eggs hatch four days after being laid. The larvae feed on ear wax and skin oil for about a week before molting into protonymphs. After feeding for another week, protonymphs molt into deutonymphs, which then mate with adult male mites. After mating, deutonymphs molt into adults. The odd thing is that deutonymphs have no gender until after molting. If a mite molts into a female, the eggs will be ready for laying. If it molts into a male, there is no sign of eggs and he is ready to mate with a deutonymph.

Treating mite infections require cleaning the ears and then applying a miticide. There are commercial ear cleaning products, but the one I like is an old-fashioned treatment made up of a 50% mixture of rubbing alcohol and white vinegar. Place approximately one to three mL of the solution in the ear and rub the outside of the ear vigorously for about 10 seconds. Step away and allow the dog to shake his head. Repeat the procedure on the other ear. Next, apply the miticide. Most over-the-counter miticides will require repeating the procedure every four days for about a month. The reason for the lengthy treatment is they are designed to kill adults, but hatching eggs are unaffected and must be treated a number of times until the ear is clear of all mites. One commercial product is Acarexx, a prescription medication obtained through veterinarians. It is designed to eliminate mites the first time and rarely requires a second application.

Ivermectin has been used for the eradication of ear mites, but it is not an FDA-approved treatment. Some topical flea applications make claims that they protect against ear mites because the active ingredients are derivatives of ivermectin.

CANINE LICE

Canine lice are so named because they are found only on canines. They are not transmittable to humans or cats, and those that live on humans and cats are not transmittable to dogs. Lice infestation in dogs living in the United States is uncommon, due to proper care and maintenance and a clean environment.

Lice tend to live their entire life on one animal, but this flat, wingless pest can be transmitted via contact with an infested dog or unclean grooming implements, such as combs or brushes. Measuring 2 to 4 mm in length and gray in color, the louse is visible with the naked eye and may appear as dirt on the dog's skin. The claws of this parasite enable it to cling to the dog's hair as it makes its way to the skin.

Mallophaga, or biting lice, have jaws for chewing on the canine's skin and scurf (skin flakes), and may be seen moving about when parting matted hair. Anoplura, or sucking lice, are slow moving, feed on the blood of the animal, and may cause anemia in severe cases. Sucking lice have three mouthparts, which retract into its head when not in use.

Indication of lice infestation may be seen as a dermal irritation, resulting in continuous scratching, rubbing, or biting at a specific area. The dog's coat will appear dry and rough, and in some cases, there may be reduced reproduction.

The life cycle is between three and four weeks, depending on the species. The female will lay up to 100 eggs, commonly referred to as nits, which are glued to the dog's hair and appear pale and translucent. In the nymph stage, the louse will have the same appearance as the adult, only smaller.

Treatment for lice may be accomplished by spraying, washing, dipping, or dusting the dog with compounds such as lindane, malathion, permethrin, or pyrethrins. Such treatment will need to be repeated within 10 to 14 days in order to kill the hatching nits. Commercial products such as Frontline, Advantix, Advantage, and Revolution may be used as preventatives.

SARCOPTIC MANGE

The microscopic *Sarcoptes scabiei* mite is not an insect, but is more closely related to the spider. Sarcoptic mange, also referred to as scabies, is a highly contagious, infectious skin disease caused by the mite burrowing under the skin of its host. It is this burrowing that causes an allergic response and creates the itchiness that the dog must scratch. If unchecked, the continuous scratching may lead to secondary skin infections, which are usually much worse than the presence of the mite. Although this mite can infect humans, it prefers to remain on the dog.

An indication of the presence of mites is the scratching and loss of hair. Mites prefer the areas around the ears, head, elbows, legs, chest, and abdomen, where the hair is much thinner and the skin more easily attainable. Confirmation of their presence can be determined by viewing skin scrapings under a microscope.

There are four stages in the mite's life cycle from egg to adult. The adult mite lives on the host's skin for 17 to 21 days. The female burrows under the skin to lay between three and four eggs. The incubation period lasts from three days to eight weeks, when the larvae will emerge from the tunnel and move about on the dog's skin until molting into the nymphal stage. There they will feed until molting again into adults.

Treatment may include anti-seborrheic or anti-itch shampoos such as Paramite, Mitaban, Amitraz, and lime/sulphur, which may also be used as a dip. Treatment may be accomplished by dipping the dog into a solution or sponging the solution over the entire dog. The dog must be allowed to air dry for the dip to be effective.

Ivermectin, though not FDA-approved for this use, is effective against mites when given orally or injected. The solution is dosed according to body weight and is given either weekly or biweekly. Ivermectin is toxic to Collie-type breeds, including Collies, Australian Shepherds, Shetland Sheepdogs, and some German Shepherds.

The topical flea preventative Revolution contains Selamectin, a derivative of Ivermectin, and is effective against sarcoptic mange mites. Interceptor and Sentinel are also effective products for the prevention of sarcoptic mange mites.

DEMODECTIC MANGE

Demodectic mange, commonly called demodicosis or red mange, is also caused by mites. There are three species of Demodex mites: *Demodex injai*, *Demodex gatoi*, and *Demodex canis*, with *Demodex canis* being the most common. It is not contagious, but it is much harder to eliminate than sarcoptic mange.

All dogs raised by their dams have this mite, but the majority do not show any outward signs or symptoms. During times of stress, either physical or psychological, or under conditions such as immune system suppression, the mite may make its presence known by cutting off the hair strand and living in the hair follicle, causing small, hairless patches to appear. Hairless patches generally begin around the eyes, face, and neck, but can appear on any part of the body.

The life cycle of Demodex mites is from 20 to 35 days. The only means of identifying its presence is via skin scrapings viewed under a microscope.

Demodex may appear in one of two forms, generalized or localized. It was previously believed that a dog showing signs of Demodex should not be used in any breeding program. That theory has been modified to accept the breeding of dogs with localized Demodex, as it indicates that their immune system is still intact. Those dogs with generalized cases covering the entire body should be eliminated from any breeding program, and it is advisable to spay or neuter them. Due to the stresses of hormonal changes, the Demodex could recur, and spaying or neutering will help to eliminate some of that stress.

Topical treatments of Amitraz every two weeks may be prescribed until there is no sign of any live mites. Although not FDA-approved for use on dogs, Ivermectin, given in prescribed amounts over 35 days, has proven to be very effective in eliminating Demodex.

INTERNAL PARASITES

Symptoms of internal parasites are a dull coat, the inability to gain or retain weight, decreased energy, and bloated stomach, and can also include a dry, hacking cough. Internal parasites, commonly referred to as worms, are generally discovered by examining the dog's feces. Observing any movement in fresh feces is a positive indicator to the presence of worms. If you suspect your dog has worms, but they are not visible in his feces, a trip to the veterinarian's office is in order. Your veterinarian will extract a harmless fecal sample from your dog and perform a fecal float test. Examining the floated feces under a microscope helps identify the presence of worms and their eggs.

There are five types of worms that are common to all dogs: roundworm, hookworm, tapeworm, whipworm, and heartworm. Some readers might question the absence of ringworm from this list. That is because ringworm is a fungus, not a true worm.

Each worm is distinctly shaped, has its own characteristics, and presents its own symptoms. The treatment for the removal of worms is the simplest of treatments; however, if left untreated, they can lead to death.

ROUNDWORM

There are four means by which a dog or puppy may become infected with roundworm.
- Consuming an animal that is carrying the developing worms
- Consuming eggs from environmental soil via grooming
- Nursing from an infected bitch
- Acquired during development within an infected bitch

The worm's life cycle begins with eggs being passed in the host's feces. The egg develops over the course of a month in its outdoor environment before infecting a new host. The egg is then ingested via grooming, hatches in the intestinal system, and burrows into other body tissues, mostly the liver. After another developmental stage, the larvae burrow into the small airways and migrate toward the lungs. This irritation to the lungs causes the dog to cough up the larvae and swallow them, where they again enter the intestinal tract, mature, mate, lay eggs, and begin the cycle again.

If the host is a pregnant bitch, the larvae will not enter the lung, but instead migrate to the uterus, where they will infect the unborn puppies. If the host is a nursing bitch, the larvae pass to the mammaries, where it will be ingested by the nursing puppies.

Roundworms consume the host's food, causing malnutrition, dull coats, diarrhea, and a pot-bellied appearance. Left untreated, these worms can cause intestinal blockages or pneumonia, both of which can prove fatal to the dog.

Treatments to rid the dog of roundworms are relatively simple by using deworming products such as:

Pyrantel Pamoate – the active ingredient in Strongid, Nemex, and Heartgard Plus

Febantel – the active ingredient in Drontal, Drontal Plus, and Drontab

Fenbendazole – the active ingredient in Panacur

Milbemycin Oxime – the active ingredient in Interceptor and Sentinel

Moxidectin – the active ingredient in Advantage Multi

Treating the dog with these products kills the adult worm. However, the hatching eggs are immune to most medications, and a second or third treatment should be performed within 10 days. Keep in mind that reinfestation is possible, as the eggs are in the soil.

I have found that worming puppies with Pyrantel Pamoate beginning at two weeks of age is very effective. Repeating the treatment again at three weeks and five weeks of age will ensure the removal of roundworm in the puppies. The nursing bitch should be treated simultaneously with her puppies.

HOOKWORM

Unlike other worms that feed on the digested food inside the host, hookworms are blood suckers. Using sharp teeth, they attach themselves to the wall of the intestines and feed on the blood of the host.

The adult female hookworm will mate and produce eggs, which are released and passed within the host's stool. The eggs hatch within the environment and develop into second- and third-stage larvae, at which time they are ready to infect a new host.

The larvae will often enter the host, including humans, by penetrating any part of the skin that is touching the ground, generally the feet. Humans are infected by walking barefoot on contaminated ground.

Once inside the host, larvae travel to the intestines, where they mature. Others travel into the lungs, where they will be coughed up and swallowed, returning to the intestines to complete the cycle.

Anemia is the most frequent sign of infection and may appear as pale gums, weakness, or having diarrhea. Young puppies are more at risk, because they are unable to make enough blood to provide for their growing needs and feed the hookworms as well.

Treatment and products for the prevention of hookworm are similar to roundworm. Remember to treat the nursing bitch at the same time as the puppies.

TAPEWORM

The adult tapeworm hooks itself onto the wall of the small intestines by its rostellum. This circular structure has six rows of teeth and resembles a hat with hooks on it. Once attached, the tapeworm will begin to grow a long, segmented tail that can reach lengths of up to six inches. Consisting of only a head, neck, and tail segments, the tapeworm feeds on the digested food of its host. The segments that make up the tail act are independent bodies, with digestive and reproductive tracts. As each new tail segment is produced, it forces the older segments toward the end of the tail, where they separate and drop off. These detached segments are the sacs that contain tapeworm eggs.

The sac is then passed from the host via bowel movements and may be seen in the stool or on the anal area of the dog. The segment is white and looks like a grain of rice, and is capable of elongating its body to perform movement. The stretching out is similar to that of a tape measuring instrument. The sac will dry out and break open, releasing the tapeworm eggs.

When hatched, the flea larvae feed on the eggs and flea dirt left behind by the adult fleas. This dirt, resembling specks of black pepper, contains the digested blood of the host. As the dog grooms itself, it swallows the fleas and infects itself, repeating the cycle. The cycle from swallowing a flea to producing the tapeworm segment is three weeks. Swallowing a flea or flea larvae are the only means of infection.

Tapeworms are not harmful to the dog, other than robbing it of nutrients, and working dogs may show a decreased activity when infected.

In addition to spotting the segments in their stool, tapeworms may be detected via a fecal examination at the veterinarian's office.

Tapeworms can be eradicated using oral medications such as Droncit, given in accordance with the body weight of the dog. Praziquantel is the active ingredient and is now available without a prescription in over-the-counter medications. The dog should be treated with the proper amount of medication and the treatment should be repeated three weeks later.

WHIPWORM

The whipworm is the smallest of the intestinal parasites and the hardest to detect. Living in the intestinal area where the small and large intestines connect, it is rarely seen. The head, which is on the smaller portion, embeds into the intestinal wall, where it sucks blood from its host. The tail, the larger and firmer portion, is the reproductive section. Unlike other internal worms, the eggs of the whipworm are laid intermittently. The eggs pass into the outside world via stool and become embryos within two to four weeks. The embryos live in the soil, waiting to find another host. Infection occurs when one of the embryos is swallowed. Total time from embryo to adult is between 74 and 87 days.

Whipworm infection generally is detected when the host begins producing a bloody and thickened diarrhea. As the diarrhea worsens, the host becomes dehydrated and mimics the symptoms of Addison's disease. Testing for Addison's will be negative and, because the egg laying is intermittent, the whipworm may go unnoticed in a fecal examination.

Administering proper dosages of Panacur or Drontal Plus will reduce the population of whipworms. However, a second treatment should be performed within 75 days of the first treatment to effectively rid the host of infection. Some veterinarians will suggest an additional treatment between the two required treatments.

HEARTWORM

Once contracted, heartworms or canine heartworm disease can wreak havoc on a dog's blood flow. It can be fatal if left untreated. Heartworms are long, white worms which can grow to 14 inches in length and live in the arteries on the right side of the heart. As they multiply, they eventually enter the heart, reducing the amount of blood being circulated to other vital organs.

In the beginning stages of the disease, there may be no outward signs presented, but as the disease becomes more advanced, the dog may display signs of tiring or heavy breathing after a minimum amount of exercise. Other signs are weight loss, listlessness, and fainting.

Microfilaria are immature heartworms living inside an infected dog. When a mosquito draws blood from an infected dog, it carries the incubating microfilaria for approximately two weeks, then deposits them into the next dog it bites, passing on the infection. The larvae migrate through body tissue for about three months as they make their way to the heart. Once inside the heart, they will continue growing into adults for another two to three months.

If detected early, most dogs can be treated successfully. The treatment is not pleasant and requires dosages of arsenic administered in three treatments. After a treatment, the adult worms die and are carried to the blood vessels in the lungs, where they decompose and are absorbed into the body. After receiving each treatment, the dog must remain calm and inactive. Rest is required to prevent the dead worms from being deposited into the lungs. Failure to treat a dog with heartworms is presenting it with a horrific death sentence.

Monthly treatments are available to prevent the growth of heartworms in dogs. Here is a list of available products: Heartgard, Heartgard Plus, Iverhart Plus, Iverhart Max, Tri-Heart Plus, Interceptor, Sentinel, Revolution, Advantage Multi, and Proheart 6.

It should be noted that Ivermectin may also be used as a heartworm preventative when administered in proper dosages. Ivermectin does not kill adult heartworms. It will sterilize and shorten the life span of the adult, but it is more effective as a preventative in a dog that tests negative for heartworm, as it does kill the microfilaria.

Collies and similar breeds, as well as some Shepherd breeds, cannot be administered Ivermectin, as it could be fatal. Always seek your veterinarian's advice prior to any home treatment.

COCCIDIA

Coccidia are single-celled microscopic parasites that are acquired when an animal grooms itself or ingests dirt that is contaminated with fecal matter. These parasites make their home in the intestines and are unaffected by worm medications. Once established within the intestines, Coccidia will cause a watery, bloody diarrhea. This loss of fluids can be life threatening, as it will quickly dehydrate a puppy or young dog. The parasite is detected via a routine fecal exam.

The ingestion of one oocyst can wreak havoc on a young intestine. As the oocyst breaks open, it releases approximately eight sporozoites. Each sporozoite enters an intestinal cell and begins reproducing. As the cell becomes full, it will burst, releasing merozoites that seek their own cells, and the process repeats itself.

Coccidia are easily treatable with a regimen of a sulfa-based medication such as Albon. Treatment is generally advised for a period of five days and is administered according to body weight. It is advisable to have your veterinarian prescribe the proper dosages.

GIARDIA

Giardia is an intestinal parasite that is infectious to both humans and dogs, and is found worldwide. The symptom of Giardia is diarrhea. The most common cause is from drinking water that has been contaminated with fecal matter. Once swallowed, the protective shell is discarded via digestion, and the trophozoites attach themselves to the intestinal lining. Trophozoites stick to the intestines with a suction cup device, but are capable of swimming to another location within the intestines.

Detection may be determined through a fecal exam within five to ten days after infection. Treatment is accomplished via use of broad-spectrum wormers, such as Panacur. A vaccine is available for Giardia, but it is not a treatment for the disease. Instead, it is used to reduce the shedding of cysts that may become attached to the fur of the animal and cause reinfection.

BORDETELLA (INFECTIOUS TRACHEOBRONCHITIS)

More commonly referred to as kennel cough, Bordetella is highly infectious and causes a harsh, hacking cough similar to that of a chest cold. There are no signs of fever or inactivity, and the appetite is normal. The only sign is frequent fits of violent coughing.

The coughing and sneezing spread the airborne bacteria, thereby infecting all of the dogs within a kenneled area. Treatment of kennel cough is with antibiotics and cough suppressants to keep the animal comfortable while the immune system eliminates the problem.

The best treatment is prevention. A vaccine is available in both injectable and intranasal applications to help prevent its spread. Most routine vaccinations include Parainfluenza, Adenovirus type 2, and canine distemper, which are all related to kennel cough. Having your dog vaccinated on a regular basis will help protect him from kennel cough. The intranasal serum is drawn into a syringe and, with the needle removed, is inserted and sprayed into each nostril. It is painless, but some dogs are reluctant to have anything placed inside their noses.

There are many other methods and formulas that may be presented by other well-meaning persons, but, unless they are licensed and qualified, it is best to seek a professional opinion from a veterinarian, as they have been trained to assist you and your dog in almost any situation. Before attempting any home remedy, including those that have been around for years, it is advisable to seek the opinion of a professional.

Diseases and Vaccines

THERE are some breeders and owners who believe their dogs do not require any vaccinations because there have not been any reported outbreaks of certain diseases in their area. The primary reason that there have been no reported outbreaks is due to a regimen of vaccinations given at regular intervals. Those individuals who refuse to vaccinate their dogs generally realize the importance of the vaccine only after the loss of a beloved pet. These are the preventative measures that should be taken. The cost of prevention is minimal in comparison to the cost of caring for an infirm dog that has contracted a disease that could have been avoided by vaccinating.

Canine Distemper – Very closely related to human measles, it is a highly contagious disease that cannot live outside of the body. It begins with an elevated temperature that may last three days and then subside. The fever will return and the subject may develop a respiratory infection or involuntary muscle twitching, convulsions, or rear quarter paralysis, after which the dog may experience grand mal seizures, including falling over, simulating a running motion, and losing bodily functions. These symptoms may be seen repeatedly for several months. Although generally fatal, those dogs that recover are immune to the disease, but have permanent neurological damage.

Adenovirus – There are two types of adenovirus, which are identified as Canine Adenovirus CAV 1 and CAV 2. Type 1, also known as hepatitis, invades the kidneys, spleen, and liver, causing cell damage, hemorrhaging, shock, and death. Dogs coming into contact with contaminated feces, urine, or saliva are subject to infection. Type 2 is the cause of tracheobronchitis, or more commonly known as kennel cough. This vaccine will not prevent kennel cough, but will limit the opportunity of secondary infection. Infected animals will have a dry, hacking cough and may expel white, foamy spittle while coughing. Dogs that are boarded or come into contact with unfamiliar dogs should be vaccinated for kennel cough.

NOTE: Adenovirus Type 2 vaccines provide cross-protection against Type 1, eliminating the need for two injections.

Parainfluenza – An upper respiratory infection with symptoms similar to the common cold. This is a contagious infection that could be a factor in kennel cough. Symptoms include chronic, dry, hacking cough and nasal discharge, similar to whooping cough in humans. Its transmission is by contact with nasal fluids distributed by an infected dog through contact or sneezing (see *Bordetella*).

Parvovirus – A highly contagious disease that more often manifests in puppies between eight and twelve weeks of age. The disease is spread by contact with urine and feces of infected dogs or the residue that may remain on grass, clothing, etc. Symptoms include bloody diarrhea, vomiting, and rapid dehydration. Without large quantities of fluid and antibiotics, death can occur in as little as 24 hours after the first visible signs.

Leptospirosis – also known as yellow jaundice, it is spread when a skin abrasion comes into contact with the urine of an infected rodent, skunk, or raccoon, or by ingestion of infected matter. Symptoms include several days of high fever that suddenly drops, extreme thirst, lethargy, and labored breathing. Vomiting may occur. Gums and eyes will appear yellow in color. Death may occur within five days.

Coronavirus – A separate virus that is unrelated to parvovirus, but similar in symptoms and treatment. This disease mainly affects puppies between eight and twelve weeks of age.

Lyme Disease – A disease spread by the bite of the deer tick. Symptoms are high fever, loss of appetite, joint pain, and swollen lymph nodes. Without antibiotic treatment, this disease could affect the heart, kidneys, and joints.

Rabies - This deadly disease is more commonly transmitted in saliva from the bite of an infected animal, but there is a possibility of transmission via inhalation. Rabies not only affects dogs, but any warm-blooded animal, including humans. It is most often seen in the dog, raccoon, skunk, fox, and bat. The incubation period is between two and eight weeks, but clinical signs of the disease may be seen within ten days of a bite. Death can occur within three to seven days after the onset of signs. Dogs that are diagnosed with rabies are euthanized.

A vaccine schedule is available for humans suspected to be infected by rabies, and includes injections on days 1, 3, 7, 14, and 28 following a bite.

Bordetella – Also known as kennel cough, is more commonly contracted when dogs are kenneled or congregate within close quarters. It is highly contagious. Symptoms are a dry, hacking cough with the expulsion of white, foamy spittle.

VACCINES

Bordetella Vaccine – This vaccine is available as an intranasal spray or as a subcutaneous injectable, and is given to provide added protection against kennel cough. The nasal vaccine is the one more frequently administered, as it provides protection at a faster rate. It appears that the nasal vaccine does not provide year-long protection; therefore, it is advisable to have it administered at six-month intervals. The injectable type takes a little longer to become effective, but provides protection for a longer period of time.

Puppies younger than six weeks of age are protected from many diseases by the colostrum they received during the first three days of nursing. Beginning at six weeks of age, every dog should begin a regimen of vaccines aimed at disease control. The vaccinations are given at two- to three-week intervals and are normally completed by 16 weeks of age with an annual booster. If an older dog is acquired, ask for its health and shot record or the name of the veterinarian who has cared for him. If the regimen was not performed, it is highly recommended that it be done, regardless of age. The traveling back and forth to the veterinarian's office every few weeks may seem like an inconvenience, but this series of vaccinations will benefit you, your dog, and the public.

Multivalent vaccines are a combination of ingredients in a single-dose vial. The combined ingredients will vary depending upon the manufacturer.

This enables the veterinarian the opportunity to provide protection against multiple diseases with the administration of one injection. Multivalent vaccines vary in their ingredients and the protection will be determined by which one is chosen. These vaccines are normally referred to as five-, six-, and seven-way vaccines. Vaccine manufacturers provide various combinations of ingredients in their vaccines, and the one chosen by your veterinarian will be the one he feels best suits his regimen.

Five-way vaccines may contain protection against canine distemper, adenovirus type 2 (includes protection against type 1), parainfluenza, and parvovirus (modified live virus, MVL, or killed virus, KV).

Six-way vaccines may contain protection against canine distemper (measles), adenovirus type 2 (includes protection against type 1), parainfluenza, parvovirus (modified live virus, MVL, or killed virus, KV), and leptospirosis, or coronavirus.

Seven-way vaccines may contain against canine distemper (measles), adenovirus type 2 (includes protection against type 1), parainfluenza, parvovirus (modified live virus, MVL, or killed virus, KV), leptospirosis, and coronavirus.

Eight-way vaccines may contain protection against canine distemper (measles), adenovirus type 2 (includes protection against type 1), parainfluenza, parvovirus (modified live virus, MVL, or killed virus, KV), leptospirosis, and coronavirus.

Lyme Vaccine – Protects against the symptoms and effects of Lyme disease. As of this writing, the federal government has granted conditional use of a vaccine developed by Fort Dodge Laboratories, is available in 43 states. Alaska, Colorado, Hawaii, and Montana have rejected the vaccine due to the small number of reported cases. California, Michigan, and New Jersey have not yet made a decision.

Rabies Vaccine – This vaccine is administered separately from all other vaccines, and is available in one- and three-year protection. Most veterinarians use the three-year dose, but some states require the vaccine be given annually. The vaccine will protect against infection, and is required by law to be given to all domestic dogs and cats. The vaccine should never be given to any wild animal.

The vaccination schedule that follows is the one most often recommended by veterinarians. If a vaccination schedule is not started at six weeks of age, the vaccines will be administered at three- to four-week intervals beginning with the first vaccine that should have been administered at six weeks of age.

Six weeks of age: First vaccination. Five- or six-way vaccine. Depending on the opinion of the veterinarian, leptospirosis and coronavirus vaccines may be withheld at this time.

Nine weeks of age: Second vaccination. Seven- or eight-way vaccine. Coronavirus is generally included in the eight-way vaccine. If a seven-way vaccine is used, it is advisable to administer a coronavirus vaccine. Coronavirus requires two injections in order to provide protection, the first of which is normally administered at this age.

Twelve weeks of age: Third vaccination. Seven- or eight-way vaccine. Second coronavirus if seven-way vaccine is used. Lyme, rabies, and bordetella vaccines may be given at this time.

Fourteen weeks of age: Some veterinarians will wait until this time to administer the rabies vaccine. They prefer separating it from the other vaccines administered at 12 weeks.

Sixteen weeks of age: Booster shot consisting of seven- or eight-way vaccine, second bordetella vaccine, and a rabies vaccination if one was not administered at 12 or 14 weeks.

Annual: At the conclusion of this regimen, you will be required to renew one multivaccine booster, rabies, Lyme, and bordetella on an annual basis.

By maintaining your dog's recommended vaccination schedule when it is due, you are aiding in the protection of your dog's health against diseases that are both communicable and deadly.

Facts About Food

WHENEVER two or more breeders engage in conversation, the topic will eventually turn to food. The majority of those discussions involve the cost of food. "How much do you pay for a bag of food?" "Where do you get it from?" "Do your dogs like it?" "How does your dog perform on that food?" "Do you see any side effects?"

The cost of food increases with each passing year, and there is always a new company boasting a new and better product, or so the advertisement says. The truth is that cost is relative to the quantity of food, as well as the quality. When checking food prices, some dog owners will overlook the fact that the bags have gotten smaller. There was a time when a bag of food from the feed store, regardless of the brand, weighed 5, 10, 25, or 50 pounds, so it was easy to establish where the bargains were. Today, foods are packaged in 50, 40, 37, 35, 33, 25, 20, 10, and 5-pound bags. This makes price comparisons a little difficult. With all ingredients being equal, you have to establish the per pound price of the food in order to determine which one is the better value. Value is not the only consideration. When choosing a food, it should provide your dog with sound nutrition, while costing the least.

Since there is nothing I can do about cost, I will present you with the facts governing the food label. Pet food labeling is regulated at two levels. The

FDA regulations require proper identification of the product, net quantity statement, name and place of business of the manufacturer or distributor, and a listing of all of the ingredients in their proper order from highest percentage to least, based on weight. Some states also enforce their own labeling regulations. Many of these regulations are based on a model provided by the Association of American Feed Control Officials (AAFCO). Here is an explanation of that model. The information that follows is taken from the Food and Drug Administration, Center for Veterinary Medicine.

INFORMATION FOR CONSUMERS
FOOD AND DRUG ADMINISTRATION
CENTER FOR VETERINARY MEDICINE
INTERPRETING PET FOOD LABELS
The following consumer information is provided by David A. Dzanis, DVM, Ph.D., DACVN.

Pet food labeling is regulated at two levels. The Federal regulations, enforced by the FDA's Center for Veterinary Medicine (CVM), establish standards applicable for all animal feeds: proper identification of product, net quantity statement, manufacturer's address, and proper listing of ingredients. Some States also enforce their own labeling regulations. Many of these have adopted the model pet food regulations established by the Association of American Feed Control Officials (AAFCO). These regulations are more specific in nature, covering aspects of labeling such as the product name, the guaranteed analysis, the nutritional adequacy statement, feeding directions, and calorie statements.

PRODUCT NAME
The product name is the first part of the label noticed by the consumer and can be a key factor in the consumer's decision to buy the product. For that reason, manufacturers often use fanciful names or other techniques to emphasize a particular aspect. Since many consumers purchase a product based on the presence of a specific ingredient, many product names incorporate the name of an ingredient to highlight its inclusion in the product. The percentages of named ingredients in the total product are dictated by four AAFCO rules.

The "95%" rule applies to products consisting primarily of meat, poultry or fish, such as some of the canned products. They have simple names, such as "Beef for Dogs" or "Tuna Cat Food." In these examples, at least 95% of the product must be the named ingredient (beef or tuna, respectively), not counting the water added for processing and "condiments." Counting the added water, the named ingredient still must comprise 70% of the product. Since ingredient lists must be declared in the proper order of predominance by weight, "beef" or "tuna" should be the first ingredient listed, followed often by water, and then other components such as vitamins and minerals. If the name includes a combination of ingredients, such as "Chicken 'n Liver Dog Food," the two together must comprise 95% of the total weight. The first ingredient named in the product name must be the one of higher predominance in the product. For example, the product could not be named "Lobster and Salmon for Cats" if there is more salmon than lobster in the product. Because this rule only applies to ingredients of animal origin, ingredients that are not from a meat, poultry, or fish source, such as grains and vegetables, cannot be used as a component of the 95% total. For example, a "Lamb and Rice Dog Food" would be misnamed unless the product was comprised of at least 95% lamb. The "25%" or "dinner" rule applies to many canned and dry products. If the named ingredients comprise at least 25% of the product (not counting the water for processing), but less than 95%, the name must include a qualifying descriptive term, such as "Beef Dinner for Dogs." Many descriptors other than "dinner" are used, however. "Platter," "entree," "nuggets," and "formula" are just a few examples. Because in this example only one-quarter of the product must be beef, it would most likely be found third or fourth on the ingredient list. Since the primary ingredient is not always the named ingredient and may in fact be an ingredient that is not desired, the ingredient list should always be checked before purchase. For example, a cat owner may have learned from his or her finicky feline to avoid buying products with fish in it, since the cat does not like fish. However, a "Chicken Formula Cat Food" may not always be the best choice, since some "chicken formulas" may indeed contain fish, and sometimes may contain even more fish than chicken. A quick check of the ingredient list would avert this mistake.

If more than one ingredient is included in a "dinner" name, they must total 25% and be listed in the same order as found on the ingredient list. Each named ingredient must be at least 3% of the total, too. Therefore, "Chicken 'n Fish Dinner Cat Food" must have 25% chicken and fish combined, and at least 3% fish. Also, unlike the "95%" rule, this rule applies to all ingredients, whether of animal origin or not. For example, a "Lamb and Rice Formula for Cats" would be an acceptable name as long as the amounts of lamb and rice combined totaled 25%.

The "3%" or "with" rule was originally intended to apply only to ingredients highlighted on the principal display panel, but outside the product name, in order to allow manufacturers to point out the presence of minor ingredients that were not added in sufficient quantity to merit a "dinner" claim. For example, a "Cheese Dinner," with 25% cheese, would not be feasible or economical to produce, but either a "Beef Dinner for Dogs" or "Chicken Formula Cat Food" could include a side burst "with cheese" if at least 3% cheese is added. Recent amendments to the AAFCO model regulations now allow use of the term "with" as part of the product name, too, such as "Dog Food With Beef" or "Cat Food With Chicken." Now, even a minor change in the wording of the name has a dramatic impact on the minimum amount of the named ingredient required, e.g., a can of "Cat Food With Tuna" could be confused with a can of "Tuna Cat Food," but, whereas the latter example must contain at least 95% tuna, the first needs only 3%. Therefore, the consumer must read labels carefully before purchase to ensure that the desired product is obtained.

Under the "flavor" rule, a specific percentage is not required, but a product must contain an amount sufficient to be able to be detected. There are specific test methods, using animals trained to prefer specific flavors, which can be used to confirm this claim. In the example of "Beef Flavor Dog Food," the word "flavor" must appear on the label in the same size, style, and color as the word "beef." The corresponding ingredient may be beef, but more often it is another substance that will give the characterizing flavor, such as beef meal or beef by-products.

With respect to flavors, pet foods often contain "digests," which are materials treated with heat, enzymes, and/or acids to form concentrated natural flavors. Only a small amount of a "chicken digest" is needed to produce a "Chicken Flavored Cat Food," even though no actual chicken is added to the food. Stocks or broths are also occasionally added. Whey is often used to add a milk flavor. Often labels will bear a claim of "no artificial flavors." Actually, artificial flavors are rarely used in pet foods. The major exception to that would be artificial smoke or bacon flavors, which are added to some treats.

NET QUANTITY STATEMENT
The net quantity statement tells you how much product is in the container. There are many FDA regulations dictating the format, size, and placement of the net quantity statement. None of these do any good if the consumer does not check the quantity statements, especially when comparing the cost of products. For example, a 14-ounce can

of food may look identical to the one-pound can of food right next to it. Also, dry products may differ greatly in density, especially some of the "light" products. Thus, a bag that may typically hold 40 pounds of food may only hold 35 pounds of a food that is "puffed up." A cost per ounce or per-pound comparison between products is always prudent.

MANUFACTURER'S NAME AND ADDRESS

The "manufactured by..." statement identifies the party responsible for the quality and safety of the product and its location. If the label says "manufactured for..." or "distributed by...," the food was manufactured by an outside manufacturer, but the name on the label still designates the responsible party. Not all labels include a street address along with the city, state, and zip code, but by law, it should be listed in either a city directory or a telephone directory. Many manufacturers also include a toll-free number on the label for consumer inquiries. If a consumer has a question or complaint about the product, he or she should not hesitate to use this information to contact the responsible party.

INGREDIENT LIST

All ingredients are required to be listed in order of predominance by weight. The weights of ingredients are determined as they are added in the formulation, including their inherent water content. This latter fact is important when evaluating relative quantity claims, especially when ingredients of different moisture contents are compared.

For example, one pet food may list "meat" as its first ingredient, and "corn" as its second. The manufacturer does not hesitate to point out that its competitor lists "corn" first ("meat meal" is second), suggesting the competitor's product has less animal-source protein than its own. However, meat is very high in moisture (approximately 75% water). On the other hand, water and fat are removed from meat meal, so it is only 10% moisture (what is left is mostly protein and minerals). If we could compare both products on a dry matter basis (mathematically "remove" the water from both ingredients), we could see that the second product had more animal-source protein from meat meal than the first product had from meat, even though the ingredient list suggests otherwise.

That is not to say that the second product has more "meat" than the first, or in fact, any meat at all. Meat meal is not meat per se, since most of the fat and water have been removed by rendering. Ingredients must be listed by their "common or usual" name. Most ingredients on pet food labels have a corresponding definition in the AAFCO Official Publication. For example, "meat" is defined as the "clean flesh of slaughtered mammals and is limited to...the striate muscle...with or without the accompanying and overlying fat and the portions of the skin, sinew, nerves, and blood vessels which normally accompany the flesh." On the other hand, "meat meal" is "the rendered product from mammal tissues, exclusive of any added blood, hair, horn, hide trimmings, manure, stomach, and rumen contents." Thus, in addition to the processing, it could also contain parts of animals one would not think of as "meat." Meat meal may not be very pleasing to think about eating yourself, even though it is probably more nutritious. Animals do not share in people's aesthetic concerns about the source and composition of their food. Regardless, the distinction must be made in the ingredient list (and in the product name). For this reason, a product containing "lamb meal" cannot be named a "Lamb Dinner."

Further down the ingredient list, the "common or usual" names become less common or usual to most consumers. The majority of ingredients with chemical-sounding names are, in fact, vitamins, minerals, or other nutrients. Other possible ingredients may include artificial colors, stabilizers, and preservatives. All should be either "Generally Recognized As Safe" (GRAS) or approved food additives for their intended uses.

If scientific data are presented that show a health risk to animals from an ingredient or additive, CVM can act to prohibit or modify its use in pet food. For example, propylene glycol was used as a humectant in soft/moist pet foods. This helps retain water and gives these products their unique texture and taste. It was affirmed GRAS for use in human and animal food before the advent of soft-moist foods. It was known for some time that propylene glycol caused Heinz body formation (small clumps of proteins seen in the cells when viewed under the microscope) in the red blood cells of cats, but it could not be shown to cause overt anemia or other clinical effects. However, recent reports in the veterinary literature of scientifically sound studies have shown that propylene glycol reduces the red blood cell survival time, renders red blood cells more susceptible to oxidative damage, and has other adverse effects in cats consuming the substance at levels found in soft-moist food. In light of this new data, CVM amended the regulations to expressly prohibit the use of propylene glycol in cat foods.

Another pet food additive of some controversy is ethoxyquin, which was approved as a food additive over 35 years ago for use as an antioxidant chemical preservative in animal feeds. Approximately ten years ago, CVM began receiving reports from dog owners attributing the presence of ethoxyquin in the dog food with a myriad of adverse effects, such as allergic reactions, skin problems, major organ failure, behavior problems, and cancer. However, there was a paucity of available scientific data to support these contentions, or to show other adverse effects in dogs at levels approved for use in dog foods. More recent studies by the manufacturer of ethoxyquin showed a dose-dependent accumulation of a hemoglobin-related pigment in the liver, as well as increases in the levels of liver-related enzymes in the blood. Although these changes are due to ethoxyquin in the diet, the pigment is not made from ethoxyquin itself and the health significance of these findings is unknown. More information on the utility of ethoxyquin is still needed in order for CVM to amend the maximum allowable level to below that which would cause these effects, but which still would be useful in preserving the food. While studies are being conducted to ascertain a more accurate minimum effective level of ethoxyquin in dog foods, CVM has asked the pet food industry to voluntarily lower the maximum level of use of ethoxyquin in dog foods from 150 ppm (0.015%) to 75 ppm. Regardless, most pet foods that contained ethoxyquin never exceeded the lower amount, even before this recommended change.

GUARANTEED ANALYSIS

At minimum, a pet food label must state guarantees for the minimum percentages of crude protein and crude fat, and the maximum percentages of crude fiber and moisture. The "crude" term refers to the specific method of testing the product, not to the quality of the nutrient itself.

Some manufacturers include guarantees for other nutrients as well. The maximum percentage of ash (the mineral component) is often guaranteed, especially on cat foods. Cat foods commonly bear guarantees for taurine and magnesium as well. For dog foods, minimum percentage levels of calcium, phosphorus, sodium, and linoleic acid are found on some products.

Guarantees are declared on an "as-fed" or "as-is" basis; that is, the amounts present in the product as it is found in the can or bag. This does not have much meaning when the guarantees of two products of similar moisture content are compared (for example, one dry dog food versus another). However, when comparing the guaranteed analyses between dry and canned products, note that the levels of crude protein and most other nutrients are much lower for the canned product. This can be explained by looking at the relative moisture contents. Canned foods typically contain 75 to 78% moisture, whereas dry foods contain only 10 to 12% water. To make meaningful comparisons of nutrient levels between canned and dry products, they should be looked at on the same moisture basis.

The most accurate means of doing this is to convert the guarantees for both products to a dry matter basis. The percentage of dry matter of the product is equal to 100% minus the percentage of moisture guaranteed on the label. A dry food is approximately 88 to 90% dry matter, while a canned food is only about 22 to 25% dry matter. To convert a nutrient guarantee to a dry matter basis, the percent guarantee should be divided by the percentage of the dry matter, then multiplied by 100. For example, a canned food guarantees 8% crude protein and 75% moisture (or 25% dry matter), while a dry food contains 27% crude protein and 10% moisture (or 90% dry matter). Which has more protein, the dry or canned? Calculating the dry matter protein of both, the canned contains 32% crude protein on a dry matter basis (8/25 X 100 = 32), while the dry has only 30% on a dry matter basis (27/90 X 100 = 30). Thus, although it looks like the dry has a lot more protein, when the water is counted out, the canned actually has a little more. An easier way is to remember that the amount of dry matter in the dry food is about four times the amount in a canned product. To compare guarantees between a dry and canned food, multiply the guarantees for the canned food times four first.

It is especially important to look at the moisture guarantee for canned foods, even when comparing one canned food with another. Under AAFCO regulations, the maximum percentage moisture content for a pet food is 78%, except for products labeled as a "stew," "in sauce," "in gravy," or similar terms. The extra water gives the product the qualities needed to have the appropriate texture and fluidity. Some of these exempted products have been found to contain as much as 87.5% moisture. This does not sound like much of a difference until the dry matter contents are compared. For example, a product with a guarantee of 87.5% moisture contains 12.5% dry matter, only half as much as a product with a 75% moisture guarantee (25% dry matter).

NUTRITIONAL ADEQUACY STATEMENT
Any claim that a product is "complete," "balanced," "100% nutritious," or similarly suggests that a product is suitable for sole nourishment that is not, in fact, nutritionally adequate is a potentially unsafe product. For this reason, an AAFCO nutritional adequacy statement is one of the most important aspects of a dog or cat food label. A "complete and balanced" pet food must be substantiated for nutritional adequacy by one of two means.

The first method is for the pet food to contain ingredients formulated to provide levels of nutrients that meet an established profile. Presently, the AAFCO Dog or Cat Food Nutrient Profiles are used. Products substantiated by this method should include the words, "(Name of product) is formulated to meet the nutritional levels established by the AAFCO (Dog/Cat) Food Nutrient Profiles." This means the product contains the proper amount of protein, calcium, and other recognized essential nutrients needed to meet the needs of the healthy animal. The recommendations of the National Research Council (NRC) were once used as the basis for nutritional adequacy, but they are no longer considered valid for this purpose. The alternative means of substantiating nutritional adequacy is for the product to be tested following the AAFCO Feeding Trial Protocols. This means that the product, or "lead" member of a "family" of products, has been fed to dogs or cats under strict guidelines and found to provide proper nutrition. These products should bear the nutritional adequacy statement "Animal feeding tests using AAFCO procedures substantiate that (name of product) provides complete and balanced nutrition."

Regardless of the method used, the nutritional adequacy information will also state for which life stages the product is suitable, such as "for maintenance," or "for growth." A product intended "for all life stages" meets more stringent nutritional needs for growth and reproduction. A maintenance ration will meet the needs of an adult, nonreproducing dog or cat of normal activity, but may not be sufficient for a growing, reproducing, or hard-working animal.

On the other hand, an all-life stages ration can be fed for maintenance. Although the higher levels of nutrients would not be harmful to the healthy adult animal, they are not really necessary. Occasionally a product may be labeled for a more specific use or life stage, such as "senior" or for a specific size or breed. However, there is little information as to the true dietary needs of these more specific uses, and no rules governing these types of statements have been established. Thus, a "senior" diet must meet the requirements for adult maintenance, but no more. A product that does not meet either of these methods must state that "this product is intended for intermittent or supplemental feeding," except if it is conspicuously identified as a snack or treat.

FEEDING DIRECTIONS
Feeding directions instruct the consumer on how much product should be offered to the animal. At minimum, they should include verbiage such as "feed ___ cups per ___ pounds of body weight

daily." On some small cans, this may be all the information that can fit. The feeding directions should be taken as rough guidelines, a place to start. Breed, temperament, environment, and many other factors can influence food intake. Manufacturers attempt to cover almost all contingencies by setting the directions for the most demanding. The best suggestion is to offer the suggested amount first, and then to increase or cut back as needed to maintain body weight in adults or to achieve proper rate of gain in puppies. A nursing mother should be offered all the food she wants to eat.

CALORIE STATEMENT
Pet foods can vary greatly in calorie content, even among foods of the same type and formulated for the same life stage. Feeding directions vary among manufacturers, too, so the number of calories delivered in a daily meal of one food may be quite different from another. The number of calories in a product roughly relates to the amount of fat, although varying levels of non-calorie-containing components, such as water and fiber, can throw this correlation off. The best way for consumers to compare products and determine how much to be fed is to know the calorie content. However, until recently, calorie statements were not allowed on pet food labels. New AAFCO regulations were developed to allow manufacturers to substantiate calorie content and include a voluntary statement.

If a calorie statement is made on the label, it must be expressed on a "kilocalories per kilogram" basis. Kilocalories has the same meaning as the "calories" that we as consumers are used to seeing on food labels. A "kilogram" is a unit of metric measurement equal to 2.2 pounds. Manufacturers are also allowed to express the calories in familiar household units along with the required statement (for example, "per cup" or "per can"). Even without this additional information, however, consumers can make meaningful comparisons between products and pick those best suited for their animals' needs. As with the guaranteed analysis, the calorie statement is made on an "as fed" basis, so corrections for moisture content must be made as described above. To roughly compare the caloric content values between a canned and a dry food, multiply the value for the canned food by four.

OTHER LABEL CLAIMS
Many pet foods are labeled as "premium," and some now are "super premium" and even "ultra premium." Other products are touted as "gourmet" items. Products labeled as premium or gourmet are not

required to contain any different or higher quality ingredients, nor are they held up to any higher nutritional standards than are any other complete and balanced products.

The term "natural" is often used on pet food labels, although that term does not have an official definition either. For the most part, "natural" can be construed as equivalent to a lack of artificial flavors, artificial colors, or artificial preservatives in the product. As mentioned above, artificial flavors are rarely used in any case. Artificial colors are not really necessary, except to please the pet owner's eye. If used, they must be from approved sources, just as for human foods. Especially for high-fat dry products, some form of preservative must be used to prevent rancidity. Natural-source preservatives, such as mixed tocopherols (a source of vitamin E), can be used in place of artificial preservatives. However, they may not be as effective.

"Natural" is not the same as "organic." The latter term refers to the conditions under which the plants were grown or animals were raised. There are no official rules governing the labeling of organic foods for humans or pets at this time, but the United States Department of Agriculture is developing regulations dictating what types of pesticides, fertilizers, and other substances can be used in organic farming.

SUMMARY

Pet owners and veterinary professionals have a right to know what they are feeding their animals. Pet food labels contain a wealth of information if one knows how to read it. Do not be swayed by the many marketing gimmicks or eye-catching claims. If there is a question about the product, contact the manufacturer or ask an appropriate regulatory agency.

Now that you understand the labeling law, let us take a look at whole versus meal versus by-product information. In the following examples, chicken will be the main food source; however, the same rules apply to any animal product used in the manufacturing of pet foods.

Chicken is defined by the AAFCO as "a combination of clean flesh and skin, with and without accompanying bone, derived from whole carcasses of chicken thereof, exclusive of feathers, heads, feet and entrails." Whenever chicken or whole chicken is listed on the ingredients label, it indicates the chicken was added without removing the water from it. A whole raw chicken contains approximately 60% water. Since ingredients labels must indicate the pre-processed weight, chicken would weigh the most, but because most of that weight is water, once processed, there would be smaller amounts of nutrients in the food.

Chicken meal is defined by the AAFCO as "the dry rendered product from a combination of clean flesh and skin with and without accompanying bone, derived from whole carcasses of chicken thereof, exclusive of feathers, heads, feet and entrails." This indicates that chicken used in the product was dried prior to being used in the process and will provide more nutrients.

Chicken by-products and poultry by-product meal is high in protein and is made by grinding clean, dry, rendered parts of the carcass (feet and heads). It can contain bones, internal organs, undeveloped eggs, and feathers that are unavoidable in processing. The makeup and attributes may be different in each batch, and lack the digestibility of meat muscle.

Rendering is the processing of waste tissue into a more useful material or by-product. It can include fatty tissue, bones, and internal organs. Parts may be acquired from expired market meats, butcher shop trimmings, and euthanized or dead animals from zoos, farms, shelters, and veterinarians, or those that were banned from the slaughterhouse or died in transit. The animals are generally beef, poultry, sheep, and pork.

There are some manufacturers and breeders who believe in providing a vegetarian diet for the dog. When the dental structure of the dog is compared to that of a human, it becomes apparent that their teeth are designed for eating and chewing animal tissue. In addition, the intestinal tract of the dog is much shorter than that of a human, horse, or sheep, indicating that the dog is not designed for digesting plant life.

There are many commercial dog food manufacturers, each producing a wide variety and type of food. Using the information provided above should help you make a wise decision on which type to feed. As stated before, the amount of food your dog should be given is placed on each bag of food. This is only a guide and should not be considered the requirement. The best way to determine the amount of intake your dog requires is to look at the dog's rib cage.

If your dog's ribs are poking out or if it appears that the skin is just a covering preventing exposure of the ribs, he is not receiving enough food and is below his proper weight. If you cannot see the rib cage at all, he is overweight and is receiving too much food. A proper intake of food and weight balance is achieved when the ribs are visible just beneath the skin.

This is the best way to judge whether your dog is receiving the proper amount of food.

All commercial dog foods have an "as fed" analysis printed on the bag. The amounts of protein and fat are just as important as the ingredients or source of protein, and aid in controlling weight gains and losses and in reproduction. For example, in order to promote reproduction, dogs should receive a regular "dry matter" (DM) diet consisting of a minimum of 22% protein. Converting the "as fed" to "dry matter" can be accomplished by removing the moisture content and dividing the protein by the remaining dry matter. Most dry dog foods contain 10% moisture. Subtract the 10% from 100%, and you are left with 90% dry matter. Divide the amount of protein listed on the bag by 90%, and you have the dry matter protein. If the food you are feeding has an "as fed" listing of 26% protein, the "dry matter" protein would be 29%. This is a good formula to keep in mind when choosing your food.

Canned food is measured in the same manner, except that canned food contains approximately 80% water, leaving about 20% dry matter. If the can supports 5% protein, dividing it by 20% leaves you with 25% dry matter protein.

Written on each bag of dry dog food is the manufacturer's recommended daily feeding, based on the approximate weight of your dog. Manufacturers cannot determine the individual metabolism levels of every dog. The general procedure is to perform a feed study on colonies of various breeds of dog to establish the amount of food required to maintain a healthy feeding schedule. This is not an absolute schedule. Every dog reacts differently to the food that is fed. Some will gain weight, while others will lose weight. This will occur within the same kennel and within the same breeds. It is best to observe your dog's coat and health condition in order to determine the proper amount of food needed to maintain each individual.

In my kennel, we use what has become affectionately known as the "rib and poop" test. By observing the ribs of our dogs, we can determine if they are of a weight that is beneficial to their health and movement. Observing the amount of poop that is on the ground helps to determine how well the food is being digested. Less poop means better digestion.

In the tests we have performed on our own dogs, it has become apparent that meal-type foods are more beneficial to the dogs. By-product foods are not bad, but there can be some digestibility issues with them. Here are our findings: When fed a meal-type dry dog food, the dogs will digest more of the ingredients and leave a well-formed but soft stool. By-product foods tend to leave a much softer and less formed stool.

Feeding meal-type products are a little more costly at about $1.10 per pound, but there is the distinct possibility that a lesser amount of food will be required to achieve the same goal weights and performance. By-product foods are less costly at about 60 cents per pound, but, in order to achieve the same results, the dog must eat more food, resulting in more poop. When considering the amounts of food to be fed and the per pound cost of both types of food, the cost is almost equal. With one product, you will feed less food and get less poop, and with the other, you feed more food and get more poop. The decision as to which food you decide to feed is yours to make, but, before making the choice of a product based solely on cost, consider the benefits to both you and your dog by spending a few pennies more.

RAW DIETS

Raw diets, known as BARF (Biologically Appropriate Raw Food or Bones And Raw Food), are touted by those using them as the best thing for your dog. BARF is a feeding philosophy and not a true method of providing nutritional requirements for your dog. Many owners end up with problems when attempting this diet.

Owners and breeders with multiple dogs lose time and money attempting to manage this diet and generally do not stick to the plan, creating unbalanced nutritional needs for the dog. Another consideration is that if the bones are not prepared properly, there could be serious injury to the intestines and the potential for bloat.

When feeding a raw diet, owners should educate themselves on the dietary needs of the dog to ensure that the proper amounts of calcium, phosphorus, and caloric intake are included. An improper balance of these could lead to growth problems, arthritis, and dysplasia.

TABLE SCRAPS

In years gone by, the dog would be fed the scraps of food left from the evening meal. This was not so bad back then because most of the food was fresher and untrimmed. Today, most meats are sold deboned and trimmed of most of the fat. Frozen foods are trimmed even more than meats bought at the grocery, and they have food coloring added to them to present a more appetizing appearance. Most prepackaged meals are proportioned with the idea of not having leftovers. The scraps from these meals are mostly useless or inedible to humans, nor do they provide needed balance to the dog's nutritional requirements.

In my opinion, the time and money it takes to prepare a raw diet and add in all the nutrients required for a healthy dog amounts to the same product as one of the commercially bought feeds that contain a meal formula. In addition, the formulation of the bag has all the balanced vitamins and minerals your dog needs. You simply open the bag and feed the dog.

On the subject of scraps, if the table food that we consume was so nutritious, then we should all look fit and trim. We do not take the time to eat what is best for ourselves, so why would you want to give it to the dogs?

General Care

THERE are parts of the dog that are often overlooked by owners, or never occur to them that they need to be checked until a problem presents itself. Here is a list of some of them, along with solutions that may aid in preventing and/or eliminating a problem area. Please understand that these are only suggestions and that you should consult your veterinarian prior to attempting to treat your dog.

EARS

Although they are in plain sight, unless they are bleeding, most owners are unaware of any problems that may be occurring inside the ears. Dirt and moisture are always present inside a dog's ear. Dogs that swim will get water inside their ears and owners believe that if they shake their head all the water comes out. If you are a swimmer, you know that swimming gets water inside your ears. You always dry your ears after swimming, so why not dry the dog's ears? After all, his ears are probably covered with that flap of skin that hangs over the opening, making it harder to dry out. Allowing moisture to remain inside a covered ear allows bacteria and fungus to thrive. Bacterial and/or fungal infections in the ear canal, called otitis, are very painful to the dog.

Some breeds have hair growing inside or around the opening to the ears. Inspect the dog's ear for this and shorten the hair as much as possible. Leaving the hair long will keep the ear moist and may aid in the cause of some of the problems mentioned.

Infections, dirt, foreign objects, or parasites are very irritating and cause the dog to constantly shake or hold his head to one side in an attempt to have the irritation fall out. An examination of the ear may reveal a waxy buildup, redness, dirt, or an odor coming from it. Fleas, ticks, and mites will nest in the warm, moist areas of the ear. In addition to their nesting, there may be a buildup of their feces, adding to the discomfort of moving creatures inside the ear.

Odors coming from the ear are also indications of yeast infections. Yeast will thrive in the moist areas of the ear, causing an itching sensation that cannot be scratched. Again, a continual, slow shaking of their head or pawing at their ear in an attempt to remove the problem is often an indication. In severe cases, the dog may whine whenever the ear is touched.

Old-timers used to put a mixture of rubbing alcohol and white vinegar in the ear to clean and aid in the prevention and removal of yeast infections, and this old remedy is still effective. Mix equal parts of white vinegar and rubbing alcohol, then place one teaspoonful (5 mL) of the solution in one ear at a time. After placing the mixture into the ear, massage the ear until you can hear the mixture sloshing inside. Release the dog and allow him to shake his head to remove the liquid. Repeat in the opposite ear.

When this process is completed, place a clean cotton ball as far as you can reach into the ear, then remove it. Continue cleaning the ear with cotton balls until you see no more debris. This process should be performed monthly.

There are many ear cleaning treatments available commercially and an equal number of products for the removal and prevention of ear mites. Each has a marketing statement as to its effectiveness, but it is best to ask your veterinarian prior to using any product or remedy.

EYES

Some common problems occurring with the eyes are debris in the eye, blocked tear ducts, mucus, conjunctivitis, cherry eye, and entropion and ectropion of the eyelid.

Debris may enter the dog's eye during normal activity. Foreign matter will become an irritant and cause a reddening of the eye. Most debris may be removed by flushing the eye with eye wash. If the eye continues to redden or appears to be irritating the dog, you should seek veterinary assistance.

Mucus, often referred to as "sleepers" and "eye boogers" by dog owners, is a combination of tears, electrolytes, mucins, and dust that forms in the corner of the eyes while asleep. Mucus fails to form during waking hours due to the natural blinking of the eye, which helps to wash the eye. Removal may be performed with the use of a tissue, followed by an application of eye wash. If mucus is allowed to remain on the eye, it may develop a bacteria that could grow into the eye.

Conjunctivitis is an inflammation of the conjunctiva, which causes the eye to redden and itch. The regimented treatment involves multiple applications of an ointment prescribed by a veterinarian. Over-the-counter products may be soothing and reduce some of the redness, but it will not cure conjunctivitis and should not be used.

Cherry eye appears as a bump inside the eye and will be very red. It is caused by an eversion of the nictitans gland, which is positioned behind the third eyelid, and must be corrected with surgery.

Entropion is the turning inward of the eyelid, causing the lashes to rub against the cornea. Ectropion is the turning outward of the eyelid, causing an irritation. Surgery is required to repair the eyelid in both situations.

TEETH

Most dogs over the age of two will begin developing gingivitis. Gingivitis is characterized as an inflammation, tenderness, or bleeding of the gums, but does not affect the deep structure of the teeth. The cause is an accumulation of dental plaque just below the gum line, and it first appears on the back teeth and canine teeth. A low-grade fever, bad breath, and ulceration or necrosis may occur in severe cases. The most common cause of gingivitis is the accumulation of dental plaque on exposed tooth surfaces. If left untreated, it can lead to periodontal disease or periodontitis.

Periodontitis is caused by plaque and forms a white film on the teeth and gums. Plaque, when mixed with saliva, turns into tartar and sticks strongly to the teeth. Feeding a dry dog food or crunchy dog biscuit will help keep plaque levels from increasing, but it is recommended that your dog receive a brushing and/or cleaning monthly.

Another problem is broken teeth. As strong as a dog's teeth appear, they are relatively soft in comparison to bone. Broken teeth are the second biggest problem occurring in dogs. Chewing on hard substances can cause fractures in a dog's teeth. The most common cause of these fractures are chewing on rocks, gravel, and cow hooves. Most veterinarians will agree that the most common cause of broken teeth occur from chewing on cow hooves.

FEET

The feet often do not get routine care and attention until the dog is limping. Check between the toes for pests, sores, or debris that may cause irritation. Be certain to clean between the toes when bathing your dog.

The pads of the feet, the underside of the foot, should be checked periodically as well. Small cuts in the pad can lead to larger problems in the future. Although the pad cannot be stitched, sores and cuts should receive attention until the wound is healed. This will prevent any infection from entering the dog's body.

Toenails should be checked to ensure that the toenails are neatly trimmed. Nails that are allowed to grow too long can become an irritant to the dog. Although those toenails may help the dog to dig, if allowed to grow too long they will become pointed and sharp. This can cause nasty cuts to a human's thin skin. Have your veterinarian show you how to clip your dog's toenails properly. The dew claw, that odd toenail that hangs higher on the dog's foot, also requires inspection and cutting. Some breeders will have them removed, especially in dogs that will be performing any field work. The reason for its removal is to prevent the working dog from tearing it off during his duties. This would causes much pain, plus the open wound would be susceptible to infection.

GROOMING

When grooming is mentioned to a dog owner, the first thing that often comes to mind is the amount of money it might take to have the dog look good. Of course, there are professional groomers who have all of the equipment and the expertise to maintain the special look of your dog's breed. Grooming, as discussed here, is a means of keeping your dog clean, healthy, and looking nice. It require only a little time to properly groom your dog. It is a matter of keeping up with what the dog needs to keep him looking like the special dog that he is. Here is some information that may help to keep your dog properly groomed.

Indoor dogs may be washed as often as once a week if the washing is followed by a cream rinse. This sounds like the dog is going to require beauty parlor treatments. The truth is that weekly washing with harsh shampoos may dry out a dog's skin, removing some of the natural oils. Dry skin will become flaky and itchy. Itching leads to scratching, and scratching can cause damage to the skin, leading to infection. The owner does not understand why his dog is always scratching, gives him a bath, and the cycle repeats itself. The cream rinse will help condition the skin and coat and prevent it from drying out, thus eliminating the need to scratch.

Outdoor dogs should be washed monthly. A cream rinse will also help their coats. Flea and tick shampoos and dips give protection against external parasites for approximately 14 days, but they do not protect the skin and coat. Continuous use of these types of shampoos could dry out the dog's skin.

Brushing your dog, whether kept indoors or out, should be done as follows: Long-haired dogs, once a week; medium-haired dogs, every two to three weeks; short-haired dogs, once a month. The brushing should go to the skin, and not just the top coat. The way to do this is to brush the coat in sections. This is referred to as line brushing. Select a section to be brushed, and brush with the grain, all the way to the skin. Take the next section and do the same thing until the entire dog is brushed. Short-coated dogs like the Catahoula also require brushing, but it is a lot easier. Simply pass the brush over his coat until all the loose hair is gone. Since you are already working with the dogs, go ahead and check those toenails, pads, ears, and tails.

I have had owners tell me that their dogs do not like being brushed. I have found that using a product called the Shed n' Blade will have your dog standing still and wanting to be brushed. This tool is similar to a hacksaw blade shaped into a curve with a handle added. It removes all the dead hair, even from short-coated dogs, and only takes a few minutes to use.

Catahoulas at Work and Play

IN the introduction of this book, I stated that conformation was paramount in the breeding of Catahoulas, and that goes for any working, hunting, or herding breed of dog. With good conformation, a dog is capable of excellent movement and the agility required in performing its task. Without good conformation, the dog will tire easily and lose its desire to perform.

Whenever I am asked the question, "What can Catahoulas do?" I always respond with, "Anything you like." You will often see breeders advertise that their Catahoulas are used for work, hunt, guard, pet, and show. Well, anyone who knows Catahoulas is aware that they can perform any of those tasks, singularly, or in combination. Simply said, "If you have a job that requires the use of a dog, the Catahoula can do it!"

Here is a glimpse of what Catahoulas are capable of doing.

WORK
HERDING – CATTLE, HORSES, PIGS, SHEEP, GOATS, AND TURKEYS

The Catahoula is at home herding almost any group of animals you desire. Their herding style is a little different than most people are accustomed to, but whether working the head or working the heel, the Catahoula will put them where you want them. These dogs are known for their assertive

Wager's Fred, Wager's Chester, and Camp-a-While's Bay Bay move stubborn cattle from the field to the pen.

attitude when working with rank, stubborn herds, but can be trained to be a little softer when it comes to more subdued herds.

In my earlier book, I stated that there is an owner using her Catahoulas to herd turkeys from barn to barn. Turkeys are moved from one location to another as they grow, and a herd of 1000 turkeys is very common. All the dog does is keep them moving in one direction while the owner opens the doors to allow them in.

HUNTING —
HOGS, DEER, SQUIRREL, RACCOON, RABBIT, BEAR, MOUNTAIN LION

To have a dog that is aware of its surroundings and the dangers involved in hunting goes a long way in assuring the owner of a good hunt. Knowing that the dog will do its job of finding, holding, and backing off when commanded is paramount in hunting. The Catahoula is comfortable with hunting any wild game. Showing the location of where game feeds or beds down for sleep helps

Baying their game in true Catahoula fashion, these three keep the hog in place as the hunter approaches.

Tumbling Run's Tucson's Keepsake climbing a tree in her attempt to reach the raccoon in a Treeing Trial.

the Catahoula identify the scent of the animal he must pursue. Although very quiet on the trail, the Catahoula will open up, or bay, meaning bark an alarm, whenever he has his game cornered or treed. A Catahoula's baying indicates to the hunter where the dog is and that the game is being held.

RETRIEVING —
QUAIL, DUCK, BLOOD TRAILS FOR WOUNDED ANIMALS

There was a time when I stated that Catahoulas were not good retrievers. Since that time, I have had a few people indicate to me that their Catahoulas will outwork a Labrador Retriever. I cannot vouch for that statement, but suffice it to say that this normally hard-mouthed canine can be taught to handle winged animals with care.

As for trailing wounded game, this is a breed that is hard to beat. The Catahoula, although a predominant air-scenting dog, will put its nose to the ground to locate the scent trail of the game he is pursuing.

Remo showing off his skills as a retriever. That's a quail he's bringing to his handler.

Abney's Texas Sun performs a search in the rubble left by Hurricane Katrina. Ja'Na Bickel is the handler.

SEARCH AND RESCUE —
LOCATING LOST OR MISSING PERSONS, RECOVERING CADAVERS, SEARCHING BUILDINGS OR DISASTER SITES, OR SEARCHING FOR LOST ARTICLES

Here is a subject that I could spend days speaking about. Having worked with a Catahoula named Ladyhawke, I can attest to the fact that these dogs will not only do the job, but will put to shame some of the more common breeds being used for this type of work. Most search groups are determined to make the German Shepherd and Labrador Retriever appear as the only breeds that can perform this feat. Not so, and I proved it with an easy-going Catahoula whose resume was almost unbelievable. It is the work of this dog and my persistence that was responsible for my becoming a court-certified expert in the fields of canine training and tracking. We worked alongside many different breeds of dogs and the question was always asked, "How does she know where to go and how does she work so fast?" The answer is that it is in them to please you and they will work their hearts out to do it.

SCENT DETECTION —
LOCATING THE SOURCE OF ACCELERANTS, NARCOTICS, OR EXPLOSIVES

This can be some very dangerous work, but a Catahoula that is trained to locate and give a passive alert by sitting quietly and waiting is indeed capable of performing this feat. Just as in SAR, the dog uses its nose to identify and locate the source; then, instead of barking and scratching, will just sit quietly. This type of alert is always good when working with explosives. Otherwise, they will give that noisy alert only ONCE!

Pumpkin Hill's Category 5 poses in typical stacking fashion after competing in the conformation ring.

THERAPY—
ASSISTING PEOPLE IN NEED

I have helped a few people teach their Catahoula such skills as summoning help when an owner is unconscious or has fallen from a wheelchair, picking up objects that have been dropped, and alerting when someone is at the door. This may not be the best dog for those needing other types of assistance, as the Catahoula is very protective and could think they were helping by not allowing others near the person in need. The right dog with the right attitude is key to this training.

COMPETITION
CONFORMATION—
PERTAINING TO STRUCTURE AND MOVEMENT

Conformation is a competition in which the dog is judged on its appearance according to its breed standard. These types of competitions are

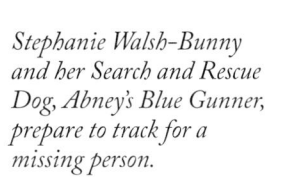

Stephanie Walsh-Bunny and her Search and Rescue Dog, Abney's Blue Gunner, prepare to track for a missing person.

seen nationally in events such as the UKC Premier and AKC Westminster. The dog is not being judged on its beauty, but is being judged on its structure, movement, and attitude.

TRACKING —
LOCATING A SPECIFIC TRACK OR TRAIL

These are competition events used to simulate a dog's task in search and rescue, Schutzhund, or any event where the dog has to use its nose to identify a specific scent.

WEIGHT PULLS —
PULLING A CART WITH PREDETERMINED AMOUNTS OF WEIGHT

This competition has the dog fitted with a pulling harness attached to a sled, sometimes soft-wheeled and sometimes on rails, with a certain amount of weight placed on the sled. The amount of weight is appropriate for the size of the dog and is increased with each passing score.

AGILITY —
ABILITY TO NAVIGATE ACCURATELY
AN OBSTACLE COURSE IN THE SHORTEST TIME

In this event, dogs perform off lead and are directed through an obstacle course by owners/handlers. The courses are designed so that the dog could not possibly perform without the aid of a handler to direct him. This requires a lot of training on the part of the handler and dog to avoid any errors.

Tumbling Run's Jaxon all harnessed up and performing a weight pull. Pulling turns out to be a fun time for Catahoulas.

Pumpkin Hill's Chasin' Shadows demonstrates his agility form.

Each dog in the competition has to navigate obstacles, such as the dog walk, similar to crossing a bridge that is 12 inches wide; crossovers; tunnels, both erect and collapsed; the A-frame; a series of jumps; weave poles; and a pause box. In the pause box, the dog sits atop a small platform for a predetermined period of time before continuing and completing the course.

This event involves performance and timing. The dog scoring the fastest time with the least number of errors is declared the winner.

RALLY —
DOG AND HANDLER MOVE THROUGH A COURSE PERFORMING VARIOUS OBEDIENCE-TYPE EXERCISES

Rally is an obedience-type event with a course that is laid out by a judge prior to the start of the event. Each dog and handler must navigate the course following the instructions that are on signs at each numbered station. For example: if the sign reads "Sit," the dog must

Pumpkin Hill's Chasin' Shadows performs a down-stay in Obedience.

107

offer a sit within two to four feet of the sign. The team then moves forward to the next sign.

OBEDIENCE —
PERFORMING A SPECIFIC SET OF EXERCISES UPON INSTRUCTIONS FROM A JUDGE

In this event, a judge tells the handler what exercises to perform. There are no signs, only the judge's spoken instructions. The handler may give a command or hand signal, but not both, and the dog must comply. The dog is judged on its performance by the judge inside the ring.

FLYBALL —
TEAM RELAY RACING COMPETITION, WITH FOUR DOGS PER TEAM

Flyball is a relay race involving teams of four dogs retrieving a ball and returning with it to the starting point. Each dog on the team must perform the exercise as fast as they can in order to be declared the winner, as these are timed events.

The flyball course consists of four jumps, the height of which is set in accordance with the shortest dog on the team. The first jump is set six feet from the starting line, and the other jumps are 10 feet apart. The ball box is set 15 feet from the last jump, which establishes the 51 feet for the course. The ball box is a device that delivers a ball to the dog when the dog jumps against it. Once the ball is delivered, the dog must turn and retrace the course with the ball. This is a fast sport, and, if you blink, you miss the whole thing.

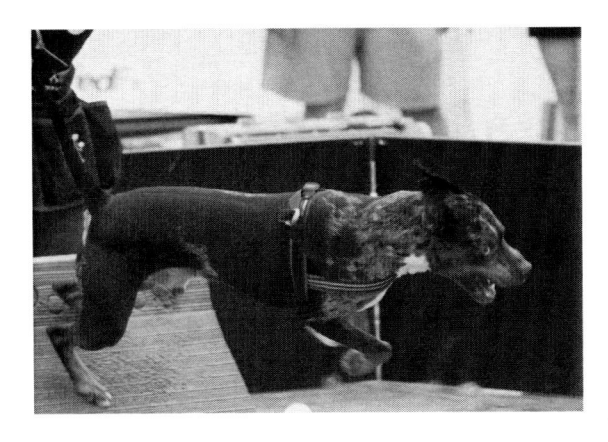

Pumpkin Hill's Chasin' Shadows is performing in a flyball event. Here he is leaping from the board on his return to the start position.

Tumbling Run's Tuscon's Keepsake flies through the air, setting a record for Catahoulas.

DOCK DIVING —
JUMPING OFF A DOCK INTO WATER IN AN ATTEMPT TO GAIN THE MOST DISTANCE

Dock diving takes place on a platform that is 35 to 40 feet in length, eight feet wide, and stationed approximately two feet above the waterline of a pool. The pool is usually four feet deep. The dock is generally covered in carpet or artificial turf in order to give the dog traction when running. The dog may be started anywhere on the dock and is then released when given a signal from the judges. The dog runs down the dock and jumps as far as possible into the water. Judging may be for height or distance, depending on the competition.

LURE COURSING —
DOGS CHASING A MECHANICALLY-OPERATED LURE

In lure coursing, the dogs chase an object around a designated track or course. This competition is similar to what is seen in Greyhound racing.

Pumpkin Hill's Chasin' Shadows stretches out to get the full extension needed in Lure Coursing.

DISC DOG —
THE DOG CATCHES AND RETRIEVES A FLYING DISC

Disc dogs follow a choreographed routine where the handler throws a disc (Frisbee) and the dog must chase and catch the disc before it hits the ground.

CARTING —
BEING PULLED BY DOG WHILE SITTING OR STANDING ON A CART

Carting can be described as a combination of weight pull and dryland mushing. A freewheeling cart containing a predetermined amount of weight, no more than three times the body weight of the dog doing the pulling, or a person weighing less than that limit, are pulled along a course by the dog.

GUARDIAN
GUARDING —
PROTECTION OF PROPERTY

Although this probably requires no explanation, when raised with a family, a Catahoula will become a natural protector and give a warning of anyone or anything that is not a normal part of its surroundings. Anyone owning a Catahoula will attest to the fact that you cannot sneak up on any property that has a Catahoula on it.

SCHUTZHUND —
PERSONAL PROTECTION

Although this is now regarded as a competition by many, Schutzhund was established in Germany in the 1900s as a means of testing German Shepherds in the art of police work. This test gained popularity with police departments and trainers and has expanded to include almost any breed of dog. Catahoulas have taken part in many of these competitions and some have completed all of the training involved.

COMPANION
PET —
KEPT FOR THE PLEASURE OF COMPANIONSHIP

After reading about all the things that a Catahoula can do, most are amazed that this wonderful working animal will be at home as a pet. The

Abney's Yankee Buck at home, thinking about what he'll get into next.

truth is when a Catahoula grows up within a household, they believe they own those people. The Catahoula can be at home in the field working, running through the woods chasing after game, or sitting in your living room with you. The most important thing to remember is that this breed requires exercise. This is not a breed you can put in a cage and forget—they will not let you.

I am sure there are some activities that I have failed to mention and that I will be receiving mail from those people who feel left out. In my first book, I made the statement that Catahoulas were not very good bird dogs. Subsequently, I received letters and pictures of Catahoulas retrieving quail and ducks. Since that time, whenever I am asked, "What are Catahoulas used for?" I simply say, "Pick a job and they'll get it done!"

Selecting The Breeding Pair

WHEN planning a litter, there are a many things that should be taken into consideration. Putting two dogs together and allowing them to breed simply for the sake of breeding, to ensure the maturity of a female, experience the birthing process, attempt to earn extra money, or for any reason other than to improve the breed, does not make you a breeder. It makes you an uninformed individual adding to the canine overpopulation problem. If breeding were as simple as putting any two dogs together and achieving desirable results, there would not be as many dogs being euthanized as there are today. Having two dogs that look good or perform well does not mean that they will produce dogs as good as themselves. Purposeful breeding takes time, patience, preparation, planning, and expense. You must be prepared for the unexpected, because, as sure as the sun will rise, it will happen. Learn as much as you can about the breed, the standard, its traits, faults, and deficiencies prior to the production of a litter.

Doing your background research on each of the dogs involved prior to breeding is of utmost importance. You should compile the statistics on inheritance, structure, temperament, ability, and color of the dogs you intend to breed, as well as those of their littermates. You should gather the same information on their parents, grandparents, great-grandparents, and the littermates of each of them. Having knowledge of the number of puppies produced in the litters, the amount of color or lack thereof, the number of deficient or defective puppies, working specimens, stamina, temperament, health, conformation, and drive will better enable you to make an informed decision on whether or not breeding the chosen candidates is the wisest thing. This research is very time consuming, but by investigating all aspects of the lineage, you will be better prepared for what may be produced from a chosen pair.

When presented with a problematic dog, I am often asked if the problem is caused by genetics. The problem is either a learned behavior or genetically influenced. Learned behaviors may be controlled and realigned. Genetic behaviors are much harder to control and cannot always be realigned.

Genes are at the core of all dogs; therefore, if there are any good or bad traits that occur, it is due to the genetic influence of the parents and their ancestors. Inheritance is also genetically influenced; however, it demonstrates a predisposition to certain characteristics. If other dogs within the same litter display the same type of characteristics, it can be said that they are predisposed to that behavior, or that they have an inherited trait. To eliminate unwanted inheritance problems in any future litters, the two dogs that created the problematic litter should not be bred to each other again. If the problem is present in just one puppy within a litter, it is probably due to a polygenic influence and very little can be done to eliminate it. An example of this is a dog that shows aggression toward other dogs, while his littermates do not show this aggression. Often, it is suggested that the dog be neutered or spayed to help eliminate the problem. Spaying and neutering will only solve this problem 50% of the time. If the problem is hormonal, surgery may eliminate the cause of the problem, but if the problem is from predisposed genetic influences created through breeding, the problem remains in spite of the surgery. Why genes align so differently in each dog within a litter is unknown.

Common traits such as type, shape, size, ability, and temperament are examples of genetic imitation known as heritable traits, or inheritance. These traits are reproducible. They give a clear indication of like genes and alleles linking together, and are easily visible and recognizable. Some heritable traits are common within all dogs, while others are seen as repetitive throughout a particular bloodline within the breed. For example, a study performed by G. Geiger in 1972 using German Wirehaired Pointers indicated that 39% of scenting ability and 46% of tracking ability are inherited traits. Note that all puppies are born deaf and blind, but locate food (the mother) by using their sense of smell. The nose of a dog, his scenting ability, is the first sense to function and the last one to fail. This is a desirable inherited trait.

Temperament, structure, and drive are also inherited traits. Maintaining those traits, even in a dog that is not used for a specific purpose such as herding cattle, will allow it to continue to possess the trait and pass it along to its offspring. A continuous introduction of dogs with nonworking backgrounds into a line of dogs will eventually reduce the working trait, drive, and spirit within that line to the point of extinction. Traits such as conformation, temperament, intelligence, ability, and drive are all important, and every effort should be taken to preserve them.

Only through careful, selective breeding can a breed be improved. Paying close attention to what is being produced to eliminate these problems from future litters will pave the way to a line of dogs that you will be proud to call your own.

Selection of your primary breeding pair should be performed with the same care as that of a doctor approaching brain surgery. Do not be in a rush to complete the procedure or skip any steps. Doing so will only present inferior results and may cause complications requiring scrapping your program and starting over. Some of the research required may seem frustrating, but do not give up. If you take the time required to complete the research, the breeding program will take shape sooner than expected. It is important to select the best specimen possible, then select a mate that improves on its weaknesses while maintaining its strengths. Evaluation of strengths and weaknesses must be performed objectively. Choosing a stud and bitch must be based on the resultant research without the influence of personal feelings.

Study the breed standard to the point that the perfect dog is pictured as it is recited. In order to picture the perfect dog, one must know and eliminate the faults. When studying the breed standard, learn all minor and major faults, as these are the factors that require elimination for the perfect dog to exist. Many breeders lose sight of this procedure by overlooking certain faults and weaknesses that require correction. Their decision to breed a dog is based solely on what they perceive as a quality trait. These types of breeders are referred to as being "kennel blind," implying that they see the faults in dogs from outside of their line, but fail to see the faults in their own.

There is an abundance of information written for selecting a stud, but the same criteria for selecting the stud applies to selecting a bitch. In my opinion, selection of a breeding pair should begin with the bitch. The reason for starting with the bitch is that she may produce four or five litters in her lifetime, whereas the stud has the potential to produce many litters with a varying number of bitches. Once you have chosen what you feel is the perfect bitch, use the same criteria to select the stud. Regardless of what accomplishments may be indicated on any performance record, ensure that both dogs display the best of their breed type, conformation, and temperament, are in good health, and complement each other's strengths. Together, these two should produce the desired characteristics in their offspring.

Place two columns on a sheet of paper and list all of the bitch's strengths and weaknesses. This will provide a guide in the search for the right stud. Whatever weaknesses are listed on the bitch's sheet should appear as strengths on the stud's sheet. Think of the strengths and weaknesses as parts of a jigsaw puzzle. Weaknesses are the missing pieces in the picture and strengths are the pieces that fit perfectly into the empty spaces. When all of the pieces are fitted perfectly together, you have a completed picture.

The first three generations of a pedigree are considered the most important. The genes in these generations are primarily the ones that will be carried forward and have the most impact on the offspring. Research on the stud and bitch, their grandparents, and great-grandparents is not enough information to make an informed decision concerning any breeding. Information should be obtained concerning each of these generations, each of their littermates, and any litters any one of them may have produced. With that said, I believe in continuing the research into the fourth and fifth generation. When weighing inbreeding coefficients, these generations will provide you with information about dogs that are related to the ones you have chosen for the production of a litter. Relationships are invaluable when used to determine the cause of an imperfection.

When researching a pedigree, you may find that a common ancestor has been used; therefore, the traits of that dog will be stronger within the pedigree. Knowing what those traits or disabilities are will aid in your decision. Just because a common ancestor appears on both sides of a pedigree does not necessarily mean it is good. It just means that particular dog was used in the breeding for one reason or another. If your research points to problems stemming from one of those ancestors, it is best to choose another dog for breeding.

This additional research can become a little overwhelming at times, but it eliminates surprises in a litter. How often have you heard, "Boy, I don't know where that behavior came from. The parents aren't anything like that." Proper research will eliminate many of those surprises.

By applying the steps presented by Carmelo L. Battaglia, PhD, in the books *Breeding Better Dogs* and *Breeding Dogs to Win* (BEI Publications), the resultant evaluations will accurately demonstrate the consistency of each inheritable trait:

Frequency of desired traits occurring among ancestors (three-generation pedigree);

Frequency of the desired traits found in littermates;

Number of carriers or affected littermates and ancestors (three-generation pedigree);

Number of pups produced with desired traits.

On a separate sheet of paper, draw up a chart indicating desired and undesired traits. List the ancestor and each of their littermates, and score the results obtained. Each ancestor and their accompanying littermates should have their own sheet. If each of the ancestors from the stud's side were in a litter of eight puppies, research will be gathered on approximately 120 dogs on that side of the pedigree. When the bitch's side is charted, another

DOG'S NAME	EYES	TEETH	HEARING	BITE	HEIGHT	CHEST	TAIL	HIPS	TEMPERAMENT

120 dogs will be researched. When all of the information is gathered and compared, a better decision can be made about whether or not this is a suitable choice of a breeding pair.

EXAMPLE

If the decision is made to use a stud from outside the kennel, research should begin approximately eight to 10 months prior to the planned breeding date. Select a few studs and perform the same research on each of them before making a choice. Selecting a stud from outside the kennel should not be based solely on stud fees, show records, or convenience. A stud fee that appears reasonable at the time may become costly in the production of the offspring if the research is not performed properly. Performance records and awards are impressive, but awards are presented to the best dog on that given day, and in the opinion of the individual making the decision. Some of the best dogs ever produced have never been inside of a show ring. Choosing a stud simply because he is conveniently located should never be the reason for his selection.

In his books and seminars, Dr. Battaglia uses "stick dogs" to illustrate this point. Draw a stick dog on a sheet of paper to symbolize the dog you want to use. Then, performing the same examination as that of a judge, examine the individual parts of the dog. Color the stick dog in accordance with its placement. Using standard ribbon award placements and colors, first through fourth place will appear as blue, red, green, and yellow, respectively. Begin by judging only the dog's head. If in your opinion this dog's head represents a winning head, color the head portion of your stick dog blue. If on the other hand it represents something less than a winning head, color it with the placement you choose. Continue examining the dog's ears, neck, front, topline, rear, and tail. Color each part with the color of your placement, respectively. When you have finished your examination and colored the stick dog, you will see where improvements are needed and have a good idea of what to do to make their offspring better.

When all of the testing, research, and examinations have been completed, and all of the blanks are filled in, you are ready to begin breeding. This may appear to be a lot of work just to get a litter of puppies, but if you are serious about producing a litter, be serious about selecting the right dogs. Perform the tests, study the results, and make an informed decision. No breeding is so urgent that you cannot take time to choose wisely.

Experience may be the best teacher, but in the case of breeding, gaining your experience through others who have already experienced the heartbreaks is better than producing a litter of puppies that no one wants. Most reputable breeders will not mind explaining their breeding techniques or discussing the art of breeding. Their concerns lie more with maintaining the breed's standard and reputation than in your becoming their competition.

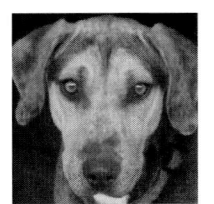

Understanding The Heat Cycle

MANY references on reproduction will state that a bitch may experience her first heat between six and 16 months of age, depending on the size of the breed. It has been my experience that a Catahoula bitch has her first heat between seven and 10 months. This cycle, commonly referred to as the silent heat, may not be as pronounced or prolonged as subsequent cycles and may even be completely unnoticeable. There may be a little swelling of the vulva but little or no bleeding, and this may last between three and seven days. After this cycle, the next one will be much more pronounced and noticeable, and generally occurs between 12 and 16 months of age. Many inexperienced owners will comment that their bitch did not come into heat until they were 16 months of age. More than likely they were unaware of the silent heat, or overlooked it.

After the first full heat, between 12 and 16 months of age and in which a bloody discharge is noticeable, the bitch will experience heat cycles ranging between six and 10 months apart. This may appear to be a wide range of time between cycles, but most Catahoulas do not cycle on a predictable six-month schedule. Many of them cycle at seven- to nine-month intervals. Still others experience a heat cycle within four months of the previous one, with a subsequent cycle seven to eight months later.

Why is the Catahoula's heat cycle so unpredictable? The answer may lie in the fact that they are so closely related to the Red Wolf. The domestic dog matures sexually between six and eight months of age and generally has two heat (estrus) cycles annually, but wolves are mature sexually between two and four years of age and have only one heat cycle annually. Wolves usually cycle and mate in the fall, when daylight becomes shorter, which provides for the birth of pups in the spring when it is warmer and food is more abundant.

The offspring of dogs that are bred to wolves are known as wolf hybrids. Studies of sexual maturity in these animals show that hybrids may mature between eight months and four years, and may have one or two estrus cycles. With the breeding and interbreeding of wolves and dogs during the inception of the Catahoula, natural hybrids were established, which also bred and interbred in the wild.

There have not been any conclusive studies concerning the Catahoula's estrus cycle, but given the studies performed on wolf hybrids, there is great speculation that their unpredictable cycles are in part attributed to their close relationship with the Red Wolf.

There are four distinct phases in the heat cycle: proestrus, estrus, diestrus, and anestrus.

Proestrus, the first phase, begins with the swelling of the vulva and an almost clear discharge. The clear to greenish discharge, lasting approximately three days, is often hard to see due to the fastidious cleaning performed by the bitch. At the beginning of this phase, hormone levels are changing, with estrogen levels rising and peaking near the end of this first stage. The clear discharge become bloody, making it easier to determine the beginning of estrus. If there are no obvious signs of bleeding, the easiest way to check for this is to wipe the vulva with a clean white tissue and examine the tissue for any discoloration. At this time, the bitch becomes very attractive to the male, but she will not allow any breeding to take place until she begins estrus. She may allow sniffing and licking of the vulva, and then turn abruptly to snap or bite at the male. She may hold her tail between her legs, depriving access, and may even chase after the male, but she will not allow him to mount.

Estrus begins approximately on the ninth day of the heat cycle and may last from three and 21 days. The ovulation phase of estrus occurs approximately

10 days after the start of bleeding, and generally lasts between five and seven days. The discharge will often change from red to a pinkish color and the flow will be diminished. As the estrogen levels begin to drop, progesterone levels begin to rise, triggering a surge in luteinizing hormone, or LH. Higher levels of progesterone are indicative of a bitch entering ovulation. During this phase, the bitch will give an indication that she is ready to receive a male by lifting her hindquarters higher in the air, moving her tail up and to one side of her body, or both. This is commonly referred to as flagging. The prime breeding time is between 24 and 48 hours after ovulation. Veterinarians can perform tests for higher levels of progesterone to determine optimum ovulation. Ovulation timing is important for a successful natural breeding, and even more important if artificial insemination is to be performed.

The next phase is diestrus, or the beginning phase of pregnancy. The bitch begins to refuse the male again and the vulva reduces to its normal size. This phase lasts between 56 and 70 days in a dog that becomes pregnant, the average being 63 days. In dogs that do not become pregnant or those that are not bred, this phase may last between 60 and 90 days.

The final phase is anestrus, which lasts between three and five months in most dogs. During this period the bitch is unattractive to males and may perform her normal activities. At the end of anestrus, the entire heat cycle begins again.

The following chart demonstrates the method of timing most often used by those intent on breeding a bitch.

BREEDING CYCLE	
DAYS	OBSERVATION OR ACTION
1 – 3	Vulva swollen and light discharge
4 – 9	Bloody discharge and bitch refuses the male
10 – 15	Fertile period. Male will mount and breed. Breeding is performed every other day until the bitch refuses the male.
16 – 28	Bitch refuses the male
28 – 32	Pregnancy tests may be performed
56 – 70	Delivery of pups
Note	Some will breed up to the 25th day, while others will not begin to breed until the 20th day

Progesterone testing may be used to pinpoint the time of ovulation. This requires a small amount of blood to be drawn and tested for a surge in LH. The bitch is ready for breeding when her progesterone levels read between 5 and 10 nanograms.

Breeding is performed every other day, because the male's sperm remain alive and active inside the bitch for 48 to 72 hours. With the sperm remaining active for this period, it is not necessary to breed every day. Having a day off from breeding may not be what the male prefers, but it allows him time to rest and rebuild his supply of sperm. As the eggs are released, the sperm penetrates the eggs and begins their transformation.

Breeding Age and Frequency

AT what age should breeding begin and end? Should a bitch be bred every time she comes into heat? These subjects have been the topic of debate since the first two breeders discussed breeding their dogs.

When questioning reproduction specialists at various universities, I found some interesting information concerning breeding. Most agree that a bitch comes into heat for one purpose only, and that is to be bred. In several university dog colonies, bitches were bred during every heat cycle, beginning with the first heat and continuing with every subsequent heat until they no longer produced a litter. There were no adverse effects to these bitches other than the loss of elasticity to the breast area. It should be noted that this can occur to any bitch, at any age, after whelping a litter of puppies. Normally the breasts will return to their original shape after whelping, but as the bitch ages and produces litters, sagging will occur. This can occur at any age or after breeding. It all depends on the genetic make-up of each individual. So, should you breed your dog every time she comes into heat? The answer is a little more complicated than a simple yes or no.

There are organizations that define the health of a dog via x-rays and testing. Breeders resort to these prior to breeding in the hope of ensuring better puppies. Some testing requires that a dog attain the age of two years prior to having certain tests performed. This waiting period prolongs the time prior to breeding, limits the number of litters produced during this waiting period, and indirectly aids in the reduction of overpopulation. All of this is simply due to the waiting period suggested prior to testing. By following the testing rules, you will not begin breeding a bitch until she is a minimum of two years of age.

Each decade gives us newer and better ways to test our dogs, which help us in determining whether there are any health risks that should be taken into consideration prior to breeding. Of course, this could result in fewer litters being produced, but it helps produce higher-quality offspring.

At 10 months of age, Catahoulas are capable of performing the same job as a two-year-old dog of another breed. However, this is only an indicator of physical capability, not mental or sexual maturity. Catahoulas reach mental maturity at approximately 16 months of age and will continue to grow and reach their physical maturity at approximately two years of age. Sexual maturity arrives between eight and 16 months of age. Some will breed a bitch at 12 months of age because they feel she is ready and able to reproduce, while others will choose to perform every test available prior to breeding. There is a middle ground for all of this. It is to study the genetic influences within the breeding pair. Perform the tests necessary to provide yourself with the peace of mind that you have done everything in your power to produce the best litter possible with a bitch that is in good health.

Research shows that a pregnant bitch has a healthier uterus than one that is not pregnant and that the possibility of pyometra is reduced. Research also indicates that breeding a bitch in subsequent cycles between two and five years of age strengthens the uterus. More recent studies indicate that breeding back-to-back heats, then skipping the next heat, is a good method of breeding, provided the bitch is in good health. Personally, I prefer to breed every other heat, with the exception that I will breed back-to-back within the first five years of age if the heat cycle occurs on a regular basis. Alternating breedings provides enough time for the bitch to fully recuperate and regain her health and stamina. It is the health of the bitch that determines the size of the litter, and one that is continuously bred will produce fewer puppies in each litter. It is better to allow her time to regain her health and stamina before breeding again. If a bitch shows any signs of stress or illness, regardless of her age, she should not be bred.

At what age should you stop breeding a bitch? That, too, is up for debate. Some registries will accept a bitch's breeding up to 12 years of age, while others recommend that breeding end between five and eight years of age. My feelings are that a Catahoula can handle a breeding beyond eight years of age. If she is in good health, capable of carrying and delivering a litter without assistance or surgery, puppies may be produced at 10 years of age. Breeding a 10-year-old bitch should not be a common practice, but it is possible.

Some breeders adopt the policy of not breeding until a bitch is three years of age. I find this to be a poor decision. In most cases, an older bitch will reject being mounted by a male. Getting an older bitch to accept a male can be an all-out fight. She may be confused by the mounting process and believe that the male is attacking in an uncommon manner, which will lead to her fighting with him. If she accepts the male, she often does not nurture her litter in the same manner as a younger one would and may reject the puppies completely.

Studies on heat cycles performed within my kennel provided some interesting results. When I questioned other well-known breeders about heat cycles, the majority of them said they just watch the attention the males give to the bitch as the first indicator that she is coming into heat. None of those with whom I spoke with had ever tracked heat cycles. After 15 years of monitoring when cycles started in each bitch, my conclusion is that there is no rhythm or consistency to the occurrence of heat cycles in Catahoulas. My study showed that some bitches had a visible cycle at 14 months of age, with a subsequent cycle between four and 10 months later, and others cycled approximately seven to nine months apart. When a bitch cycles nine months apart, it becomes very difficult to skip a heat between breedings, as she will only cycle once each year. The best advice that I can offer in these situations is to monitor the heat cycles and the health of the bitch. In other words, pay particular attention to heat cycles and make observations of what is actually going on in your kennel. Observation and health will pay off in the long run.

The frequency with which you breed is a decision that must be made by you. Regardless of your decision, ensure that all of the puppies will be placed in homes before you begin the breeding process. Do not breed unless you have a minimum of six clients who have placed a deposit for a puppy. Any bitch that is not going to be used for your breeding program should be spayed.

Males have the ability to reproduce at approximately 10 months of age, but their sperm count is so low that it is not always a successful breeding. It is best to wait until the male is over one year of age prior to using him as a stud. Males can reproduce as long as their sperm count is at an acceptable level, which is determined by genetic predisposition or age. Males may be used for breeding until they stop producing litters. Any male that is not going to be used for breeding should be neutered.

In conclusion, it is my opinion that bitches that are to be used for breeding should not be bred until they are a minimum of 14 months of

	AGE COMPARISON CHART — HUMAN TO DOG			
HUMAN	DOGS			
	UNDER 20 LBS	20 – 50 LBS	50 – 90 LBS	90+ LBS
1	15	15	14	12
2	23	24	22	20
3	28	29	29	28
4	32	34	34	35
5	36	38	40	42
6	40	42	45	49
7	44	47	50	56
8	48	51	55	64
9	52	56	61	71
10	56	60	66	78
11	60	65	72	86
12	64	69	77	93
13	68	74	82	101
14	72	78	88	108
15	76	83	93	115
16	80	87	99	123
17	84	92	104	
18	88	96	109	
19	92	101	115	
20	96	105	120	

age, proper preliminary testing has been performed, and heat cycles have been studied. The health of the bitch is paramount. All breeding should be stopped when the bitch is approximately eight years of age, give or take one year. Breed subsequent heats within the first five years if the bitch has regulated cycles, is in good health, and has completely recovered from her last litter. The bitch must be in good health prior to any breeding.

The aging process is accelerated in dogs; however, the idea that a dog ages seven years for each human year is an estimate only. This is based on the average lifespan of dogs as compared to humans. As medical care and overall health has improved, we humans have been able to extend our lifespan. Likewise, improvements in food and medicine have extended the lifespan of the dog, but not to the extent of humans.

The chart on the preceding page indicates the approximate ages of dogs in comparison to humans, based on the dog's body weight. The size of the dog has a bearing on how it ages. Smaller dogs mature more rapidly in their early years, then the aging process slows. In the larger breeds, aging is slowed in the early years and increased after five years.

Considering that a Catahoula falls within the 50- to 90-pound range, and based on the age comparisons, would you want to see a 14-year old parent?

The natural aging process is the best reason to wait before breeding your bitch.

Breeding Styles

THERE are three distinct styles of breeding: inbreeding, line breeding, and outcrossing. Each has its place in the production and improvement of a pedigree, or line, of dogs. Knowing how and when to use each can be very valuable. Written here are the basic steps and how they are used. There is a wealth of information available on this subject and varying ideas on the role of each. It is essential to understand the methodical steps required in perfecting a specific line of dogs. The breeder must be dedicated to the breed, open to new ideas, willing to share their own ideas, and take the necessary steps to demonstrate their beliefs.

Inbreeding is the breeding together of closely related specimens and is widely accepted as being parent to offspring, siblings, half-siblings, aunt to nephew, or uncle to niece. Many breeders will stay away from inbreeding based on the myth that this type of breeding will produce hideous offspring. In truth, inbreeding strengthens and supports a given line. Proofing a line by inbreeding doubles all of the genetic properties. In other words, any weaknesses or strengths that were hiding within the line will be displayed in the offspring. Inbreeding demonstrates to the breeder the areas within the line that are strong and desirable, as well as those that require correction. It may also mean that the breeder will have to keep an entire litter of puppies until they are adults before any determination of faults or successes may be determined. Inbreeding has been referred to as a quick fix to defining a specific line. Problems with inbreeding occur when it is repeatedly used within the same line. Continual inbreeding of the same line will produce weaker pups and over time, conditions may develop that were not present in the first litter. Inbreeding will double both the good traits and unwanted ones within the offspring. Thus, inbreeding may be used when improving a line for temperament, disease, function, etc. In a study performed by Vicki Myers-Wollen at Cornell University, it was proven that as the inbreeding coefficient rises, fertility and the number of puppies produced decreases, while neonatal deaths increases.

Line breeding is the breeding together of more remote relatives, such as grandparent to grandchild or cousin to cousin. Some breeders object to line breeding, stating that it produces defective puppies. In spite of that, when speaking with them about their line of dogs, they will flaunt a particular dog of some value to them appearing more than once in the pedigree. If the valued dog appears more than once in a five-generation pedigree, the dog belonging to that pedigree is the result of line breeding. Many breeders are line breeding without knowing it. Without performing the required research, they may never know which dogs are related to each other. Line breeding, or inbreeding once removed, is considered a safe fix due to the genetic influence of genes coming from a different line. Line breeding presents the same results as inbreeding but they take longer to prove and are considered safer by some breeders. Line breeding can be a little confusing, but do not let it deter you. This method has worked for top breeders for many years. Lloyd C. Brackett, better known as "Mr. German Shepherd," applied his system of breeding to produce 90 champions over the course of 12 years, a record that still stands. The basic formula he preferred can be stated as follows, "Let the sire of the sire become the grandsire on the dam's side," or, "let the father's father be the dam's grandfather."

Outcrossing is the breeding together of dogs with no common ancestors in the first five generations. This is considered safe because there are no related dogs or ancestors in the line, and unrelated dogs being bred may reduce the possibility of disease or genetic flaws from affecting the offspring. Unfortunately, this is only true in the first generation. Subsequent generations will display hidden flaws and diseases. By continually outcrossing, the breeder's line is never proven or improved. The lack of research prior to breeding may have the breeder unknowingly using related dogs. A three-generation pedigree will list the dogs in that line, but unless it is researched further by the breeder, there is no way to be certain that the dogs are unrelated. Uncles, aunts, and cousins can go undetected unless the line is researched.

Outcrossing can be useful for the breeder if used correctly. If there is a specific fault or deficiency that cannot be corrected within the line, it is best to find a dog from outside of the line to aid in correcting the problem. Keep in mind that there could be underlying problems that are being introduced. Again, research is the key.

Every breeder should own a copy of the books *Breeding Better Dogs* and *Breeding Dogs to Win*, both by Carmelo L. Battaglia and available from BEI Publications. Study and practice the methods described and you can rest assured you will become a better breeder with a better line of dogs.

Regardless of the method chosen, when it is used, or how it is used, research must be performed on all of the participants. Be an informed breeder.

Breeding Methods

THERE are two methods of breeding: natural and artificial insemination (AI). Both have variations in their procedure. Knowing the methods and procedures will provide the breeder with a variety of options by which to attain a successful breeding.

Natural insemination occurs when the stud mounts and penetrates a willing bitch that is ovulating, then deposits semen within the reproductive tract, where the sperm cells travel through the cervical canal to the uterus. It is recommended that mating take place every other day during ovulation. Allowing a chosen pair to breed naturally is always the best option, but the bitch may be unwilling or inexperienced and will have to be held in place while the stud proceeds with the mating. This can be a bit tricky, as some bitches will fight, and the risk of being bitten is increased. To prevent any biting injury to yourself or the stud, a muzzle should be placed on the bitch. Next, sit on the ground facing the opposite direction as the bitch, place your arm around her neck, across her chest, and hold the front leg nearest you. If she attempts to sit, you may have to hold her up with your opposite hand while the stud mounts. After breeding for the first time, most bitches will become a willing partner with the next mating.

If attempts to hold her in place are unsuccessful, the alternative is artificial insemination, for which there are four options.

Fresh semen is first collected from the chosen stud. The semen is then placed in a syringe and inserted into the vagina, just in front of the cervix. Once the semen is in place, the abdomen is palpated to aid the cervix in pulling in the sperm. After palpating her abdomen, her rump must be elevated for approximately 15 minutes to prevent drainage. When this has been completed, she should not be allowed to jump or urinate for approximately 45 minutes, after which normal activities may resume. Fresh semen may live up to eleven days and has the ability to fertilize eggs for about five to six days.

Chilled semen is a method of acquiring semen from a desired stud that may be located too far away to make natural breeding possible. Semen is collected from a stud and a solution is added to aid in cooling it down. The semen is then shipped to the location where it will be activated and used in the same manner as an AI with fresh semen. Using chilled semen requires progesterone testing to determine the time of ovulation. Chilled semen may live up to five days, shortening the fertilization period.

The next two procedures address AI using frozen semen. Semen is drawn from a stud, placed in 0.5-mL straws, and frozen in liquid nitrogen at -196 degrees Centigrade. When ready for use, it is shipped, thawed, and inserted. Frozen semen must be implanted within the uterus within 48 to 72 hours after ovulation. When using frozen semen, ovulation timing is of utmost importance. Progesterone testing will be performed every other day to determine ovulation. When the timing is right, the semen is shipped, thawed, and surgically implanted into the uterus by means of a needle and syringe. Once thawed, the frozen semen is only viable for a few hours, but since the semen is implanted directly into the uterus, the sperm

SUCCESS RATES OF VARIOUS BREEDING METHODS	
METHOD	SUCCESS RATE
Natural breeding with three breedings per cycle	80 – 95%
AI using fresh semen	60 – 90%
AI using chilled semen	55 – 80%
AI using frozen semen surgically deposited into the uterus	50 – 75%
AI using frozen semen deposited into the vagina	35 – 50%

are able to penetrate immediately and are not dependent upon long life. This procedure must be properly timed in order to be successful.

The other method is to thaw the frozen semen and deposit it into the vagina, using the same procedure for fresh or chilled semen. The veterinarians that I have consulted all agree that this is the least successful method.

The chart on the preceding page presents the percentage rate of successful pregnancy using each method. The percentages listed are approximated and are not to be viewed as exact.

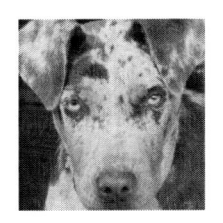

The Breeding

Dogs that are paired for breeding should undergo a brucellosis test seven to 10 days prior to being bred. Brucellosis is a canine venereal disease that affects male sexual organs and female reproductive organs, which can lead to infertility in both. The disease is spread by contact with urine, feces, semen, vaginal discharge, aborted puppies, or other body secretions. There is no known cure for brucellosis and the majority of dogs that contract the disease are euthanized.

Signs of brucellosis in females include enlarged lymph nodes, abortion of the litter between 45 and 55 days of breeding and with a vaginal discharge lasting several weeks after the abortion, birthing of dead pups, pups dying shortly after birth, or absorption of the litter, leaving the breeder with the thought that the breeding did not take.

Males with brucellosis may have enlarged lymph nodes, swollen scrotal sacs, inflamed prostates, testicular atrophy, abnormal sperm, or poor sperm motility. Males may be reluctant to breed because of pain in their sexual organs.

When the bitch begins ovulating, she should be brought to the male. Bringing her to him helps to relax the male, as he is familiar with his territory and will be a more willing participant in the breeding. If the male is brought to her location, he may want to spend his time marking what he perceives as his new territory and ignore her.

At their first meeting, the male will sniff and lick the bitch's face, then turn to sniff and lick her vulva. Depending on the attitude of the bitch, she may run off and have the male chase after her. There may be some bowing, rolling, posturing, and spinning by both of them before they get down to business. This action is referred to as the dance (Figures 1 & 2). The male will dance and strut around in an attempt to impress the female.

Figure 1

Figure 2

When they have completed their dance, the male will again lick her vulva. If the bitch is ready, she will signal him by moving her tail to one side or the other. This is called flagging (Figure 3), which is her way of signaling to the male that she is ready to breed. At this point, the male will assume the position atop the bitch's back and hold both sides of her rear quarters with his front legs as he begins his mount (Figures 3 and 4).

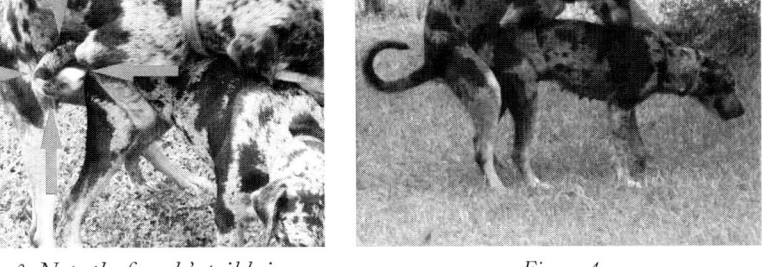

Figure 3 Note the female's tail being held to one side.

Figure 4

From this position, the male thrusts forward to locate the vaginal opening with his penis. When he successfully penetrates, his thrusting will become more rapid and powerful. As he begins to ejaculate, the bulbus glandis, or knot, on his organ will enlarge, resulting in the tie (Figure 5). Once tied, the male dismounts and passes his rear leg over the back of the female so that they are standing back to back, which places the male's organ at a 180-degree angle.

Figure 5

While in this position, pressure is applied to the bulbus, causing more ejaculate to be dispensed. The pair stays in this position until the bulbus relaxes and allows them to separate. A tie may last between ten minutes and one hour. Caution must be observed while in the tied position. Any disruption, outside interference, fighting between the two, or forceful pulling apart could twist the male organ and cause injury. Serious damage to the male's penis could result in internal bleeding and the death of the male. Once the pair has separated naturally, they will begin to clean themselves. At this point, they should be placed in separate enclosures to prevent the male from attempting another mating.

Although the tie is a good indicator that the mating was successful, a tie is not necessary for a successful mating. If the male is able to penetrate and ejaculate, the sperm that is deposited will perform in the same manner as if there was a tie.

The time to begin breeding is between the 10th and 15th days after the start of bleeding. The optimum time is 48 hours after ovulation; however, unless progesterone tests are performed, the ovulation time is a guess. Once breeding begins, the bitch should be bred every other day. It is not necessary to have a breeding every day, because the sperm remain active for 48 to 72 hours. This provides ample opportunity to fertilize the eggs and allows a day of rest for the male. Continue breeding on alternate days until the male is rejected by the female.

There are a few reasons why a bitch might not allow a male to mount during her heat cycle. She is inexperienced and does not know what to do. Having a male climb on her back may have her believe that she is being reprimanded or under attack, or she may believe he is playing. In any case, it will require time and patience in handling this situation. Attempts to calm her may not be successful and a forced breeding or AI may be required.

She may not be ready to breed. Watch for flagging. If she is not flagging, then she is not ready. A bitch will breed only when she is ready; otherwise, she will viciously chase off the male. If you are certain that you have timed the cycle correctly and she still does not wish to breed, forced breeding or AI is the only other means available.

Another reason, which may seem odd, is that she may not like the male you have chosen. In a kennel situation, the bitch will know all the males present. She also knows which are submissive and which are assertive. A bitch will generally reject a submissive-acting male and prefer one that is more assertive. For this reason, whenever breeding to a male that is not a member of your kennel, the bitch should be brought to the male. This places the male in a position of assertiveness because he is in his territory, and due to the lack of interaction on a regular basis, he should not be intimidated by the bitch.

Before attempting any forced breeding or AI, it is best to have a progesterone test performed by your veterinarian. It may require bringing the bitch to him every other day to determine the proper timing, but it is better to get it right when attempting either of these procedures. Attempting to force-breed a bitch that is not ready can be compared to shoving butter down a bobcat's throat with a hot poker. It is not going to happen and someone is going to be bitten!

Pregnancy
Care and Feeding

AFTER the breeding takes place, there is the uncertainty of pregnancy until the bitch begins to show signs of being pregnant. Methods used to determine pregnancy are palpation, ultrasound, x-ray, and chemical pregnancy tests. The majority of these can be performed after the 21st day following breeding. When two or more breedings occur, there is no method of determining which one was successful. Each of the breedings must be counted and tests must be performed at the proper elapsed time after the last breeding.

Palpating the abdomen is the most common method of determination. The veterinarian pushes up and in on the abdomen in an attempt to detect any uterine swelling. This procedure is generally performed between 21 and 35 days after the first breeding.

Ultrasound uses sound waves to produce a visual picture, from which a determination of pregnancy can be made. It provides the operator with the ability to determine the approximate number of puppies conceived. This test is usually performed after day 25 of the first breeding.

X-rays may be taken to determine pregnancy and the presence of puppies, but, because of insufficient mineralization of the puppies' skeletal structure, this procedure must be performed between 42 and 52 days after the first breeding.

Canine pregnancy tests involve drawing a minimal amount of blood to determine the presence of a hormone called relaxin, which is only present in a pregnant bitch. This test may be used 22 days after breeding, but a better determination can be made at 31 days. The test is inexpensive and can determine pregnancy, but not the number of puppies conceived.

The gestation period is 63 days, plus or minus seven days. During the first 30 days of gestation, the bitch should be allowed to resume her normal activities and food intake. Some bitches will continue to have a discolored vaginal discharge after breeding. This is normal and should not be of any concern. After 30 days, care should be taken to avoid any rough playing that could cause injury to the growing puppies. Pregnant bitches have increased energy, and exercise should be allowed and encouraged, but caution must be taken to avoid any injury. Long walks or running in a confined area are good exercises.

In the beginning of the pregnancy, there are few visible outward changes. However, by the sixth week, the mammary glands and nipples will begin swelling and may change color. The stomach will enlarge in the seventh week, and by the eighth week, the mammary glands will contain some milk. If milk appears on a nipple, just wipe it with a clean, damp cloth. Do not medicate or make any attempt to stop the flow, which should only be a few droplets. Old-time breeders would squeeze a bitch's nipples to detect the presence of milk. This practice should be avoided. Breaking the seal before it is time for a puppy to nurse removes some of the colostrum and opens a path for bacterial infection. If an infection is contracted through an opening in the mammary, it could affect the entire milk supply and harm the puppies. The importance of not breaking the seal cannot be stressed enough.

In a puppy's first feeding, he is provided with colostrum, a natural substance that promotes health, strength, and resistance to disease. After the second day of feeding, colostrum is no longer present in the milk. Because the colostrum is only present for one day, it is very important for the puppies to receive that first-day feeding.

FEEDING DURING PREGNANCY

You should be feeding your dog a high-quality, meat-based protein food with a minimum of "as fed" protein of 24% in order to promote reproduction. After breeding, the bitch should eat food containing 30% protein and 20% fat. An effort should be made to use the same brand of food, but select one of higher quality. It is always better to remain with the same brand of food than it is to switch brands, as it reduces the amount of internal stress. Continue feeding the same quantity of food with the same regularity. About four weeks after the breeding date, begin increasing her food intake in weekly increments of 10% until you are feeding one and a half times as much food as you were for her normal maintenance. For example, if she was eating four cups of food a day, begin increasing her food until she is consuming six cups of the higher-protein food. It is also advisable to begin feeding half of the required amount twice each day. This should satisfy her hunger, feed the growing puppies, and promote milk production.

After whelping, again increase her food in increments of 10% until you have doubled her normal feeding. Remember, she is feeding puppies and herself, so doubling the food is a good reference point. Food plus water make milk, and she needs to produce enough to nourish all of the puppies.

When the puppies begin eating solid food, do not cut back on the bitch's food. Allow her to continue eating the higher amounts of food and feeding the puppies. When it becomes apparent that she is producing more milk than is being consumed, you may begin cutting back at weekly increments of 10%, but do allow her to continue to nurse the puppies until they are ready to leave the kennel.

As the puppies depart the kennel, the bitch will reduce the amount of milk required to feed those remaining. When all of the puppies are gone and there are none left to nurse, continue to feed the higher-protein food for another two weeks. Then start reducing her intake by 10% each week until she has reached her normal feeding amount, and then make the switch back to her normal food. Feeding in this manner will help to maintain her nutritional requirements and speed recovery time.

The debate on whether or not to add supplements to a diet will continue until there is scientific proof about which of these opinions is correct. It is my belief that supplements are not required if you are feeding a high-quality food. The nutrients in the food should be adequate to support your dog's health and pregnancy. If dietary supplementation is required, then the bitch is not healthy enough for breeding. Adding supplements to a diet also has the distinct possibility of creating more problems in a pregnancy than providing benefit. There is no scientific proof supporting the benefit of adding supplements to a pregnant female's diet.

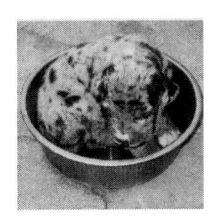

Whelping

WHELPING is the term used for a bitch giving birth to her pups. A minimum of two weeks prior to whelping, a whelping box should be prepared. Whelping boxes may be purchased through pet catalogs and pet stores, or you may want to build your own. The purpose of the box is to provide a safe area for the bitch to build her nest and whelp her pups.

A whelping box may be built from half-inch plywood and 2 x 4 lumber. The box should measure a minimum of 36 inches x 36 inches, with its walls standing a minimum of 12 inches in height above the box floor. The box must be big enough for the bitch to lie down and stretch during whelping. Some will just sit, but if they decide to lie down, they will need the space to do so. An opening on one side for easy access is optional. When the pups are born, temporarily close off the opening to prevent the puppies from falling out of the box. A rail should be placed around the inside of the box, approximately four inches from the box floor and about the same width out from the walls. Again, 2 x 4 lumber works very nicely for this purpose. Place a piece of a 2 x 4 on its edge, approximately two inches from the inside wall of the whelping box. This will give you a guide to the rail height. Now, take the board you are using for the rail and mount it to the box with screws. Do the same on all 4 sides of the box. The rails will provide a protective space for puppies to roll under and avoid having the bitch lie on top of them. The edges where the floor and walls meet should be sealed to prevent any fluids from getting between the floor and walls. The floor should be painted with a minimum of two coats of a flat, water-based paint to prevent whelping fluids from soaking into the wood. Your box is now ready to use.

Shredded newspaper or other absorbent material should be used to cover the floor of the whelping box. The bitch should be placed in the area of the whelping box to allow her time to make her nest and arrange it the way she wants. Regardless of what material you use in the box, rest assured that she will rearrange it to suit herself.

Prior to whelping, you must prepare a location where the bitch and her whelping box will be kept. The whelping box should be placed in an area that is dry, warm, secluded, and away from any drafts. Newborn puppies are unable to shiver or regulate their body temperature and must be kept warm. Shivering creates goosebumps, which trap warm air between them, and is a means of keeping warm. Without the ability to shiver, any draft will chill the puppy and may result in death. The whelping box should have an external heat source, such as a heater. Maintain a temperature of 85 to 90 degrees for the first five days, then, gradually decrease the temperature to 80 degrees between days six and 10. After 10 days, the temperature may be reduced to 75 degrees. Direct the heat source to one corner of the box, so that the puppies may move about and find the area most suitable to them. Puppies will lie on top of one another and change positions repeatedly to aid in regulating their body heat. Do not use a heat lamp. They can actually produce too much heat and the puppies may become dehydrated.

Prior to delivery, make sure to have your veterinarian's telephone number readily available, as well as the telephone number for an emergency veterinary service if there is one in your area. You might also stock up on these supplies, which could be needed:

- A 3 mL syringe or suction bulb to be used to extract fluid from the mouths and noses of the puppies
- Several clean towels to be used for drying the puppies
- Dental floss or sewing thread to tie off umbilical cords
- A pair of blunt-tipped surgical scissors or fingernail scissors for cutting umbilical cords
- Iodine to be applied to the umbilical cords.

As the arrival time nears, 12 to 24 hours before beginning her labor, the bitch may stop eating and will attempt to purge her system by defecating as much as possible. Her temperature will drop one or two degrees from normal. A rectal thermometer is used to take this reading. If you do not have a rectal thermometer, try placing the dog's ear against your cheek. The ear will feel extremely cold.

When labor begins, the bitch may show signs of anxiety and pace back and forth, or she may continuously sit or lie down, and then immediately stand up. As the labor intensifies, she will start having contractions and at this time, may show signs of straining. She may be standing, seated, or lying down when the first puppy is delivered. The puppy generally is ejected with a single push after it appears in the vaginal opening. Puppies usually are delivered head and feet first, but if this is reversed, it is of no significance.

The newborn puppies are encased in a thin, membranous sac. As each pup is delivered, the bitch will lick and bite at the membrane until it is broken. She eats the membrane and then licks the puppy to clear its mouth and nose of fluid. She bites the umbilical cord to sever it, and continues licking the puppy. This licking helps the puppy's breathing and dries it off. Within a few moments of the delivery, the placenta will be expelled and the bitch will eat this as well.

This continues until all of the puppies are born. The puppies usually arrive approximately 15 to 20 minutes apart. With large litters, the bitch may take a break, without any puppies being delivered for 30 minutes to one hour. If there are no puppies born between one and one and a half hours and she is showing signs of contractions, contact your veterinarian and make preparations to bring her and the puppies to the vet's office.

Often, when a first litter is delivered (and with some anxious bitches), they will ignore the puppy after it is delivered. If this happens, you have to help by breaking the sac surrounding the puppy. After removing the sac, present the puppy to the bitch for cleaning. If she continues to ignore it, suction out the fluid from the nose and mouth with the syringe or suction bulb. Next, begin drying and rubbing the puppy to help it breathe. Do not be concerned about any fluid inside the whelping box; your main concern is to get the puppy dry, warm, and breathing. Now, tie off the umbilical cord about an inch from the abdomen, pinch the cord flat, and cut off the sac. Place a drop of iodine on the end of the cord.

Once the puppy is breathing and moving around, put it in the box and get ready for the next puppy. On occasion, the bitch will try to leave the box with the new puppy in it. She will be scared and confused with what has happened and want to get away, but you must keep her there.

When she has calmed down and begins to accept the puppies, place them next to a nipple so they can start nursing. This first nursing is the most important, so you must encourage the bitch to nurse the puppies. In the first feeding, between 12 and 24 hours, the nursing puppies will receive colostrum, which contains antibodies that protect the puppies from infectious diseases during the first four to six weeks of life. If she rejects the puppies, be persistent and continue placing each one next to a nipple. When she begins nursing one puppy, generally she will allow the rest of the litter to nurse. If this does not happen, you will have to tube feed the puppies every two to three hours until they are able to eat soft food.

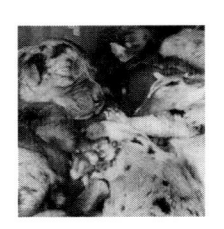

Post Delivery

After birthing a litter of puppies, the bitch may not eat for 24 hours, after which she will be ravenous. Start feeding her the same amount of food as you did during the pregnancy. Within two weeks of birthing the pups, she will require another increase, possibly as much as three times her normal intake. She is feeding puppies and herself, so her food requirement will increase.

Fresh water should be available to her at all times. Replenish the supply every day. It requires food and water to make milk, so give her what she needs.

After whelping, the bitch may have a colored discharge, which may display itself as a bright to deep red, brown, or greenish color. This discharge may last as long as eight weeks. This is a normal occurrence and is not cause for concern. However, any severe discharge or one that persists beyond eight weeks will require a veterinary examination.

WEEK ONE

At birth, puppies cannot regulate their body temperature, so it is imperative to maintain a warm place for them. A constant temperature of 85 degrees is recommended. Do not allow them to be chilled in any way.

During the first 10 days of life, a puppy does not have the ability to shiver, which is a means of controlling their body heat. Shivering causes the skin to dimple, commonly known as chicken skin or goosebumps. The dimpling traps warm air between the bumps, which aids in regulating their body temperature. Since they cannot do this, keep those puppies warm.

For the first three days of a puppy's life, I will check on the puppies and bitch to ensure that all is going well and that none of the puppies are in distress or have died. I do not interfere with the litter or handle the puppies at that time unless absolutely necessary, such as removing a dead puppy from the litter. I believe in giving the puppies time to adjust to their new environment before handling them. After three days, I begin touching, picking up the puppies, examining them for physical complications, checking their sex, and touching all body parts, especially their feet. This examination is performed while the pups are still in the whelping box, so mama, the puppies, and I are all piled into the box.

Newborns are deaf and blind, but their sense of smell is functioning and that helps them in finding the source of food. If any show signs of failing or do not gain strength within the first two to three days, begin tube or bottle feeding with a commercial milk replacement formula. Do not remove the puppy from the whelping box, but provide additional feedings while allowing it to remain with its littermates. It is not uncommon for one or two puppies in the litter to perish. There is no reason for alarm unless there are more than two losses. There is no explanation available as to why this happens, but it must be accepted that it can occur. As was explained to me some years ago, when most humans have more than eight children, in all likelihood, there was a child lost before or immediately after being born.

Once the puppies complete their first week of life, they are usually stable. There should not be any loss of puppies unless they are chilled or catch a disease.

At 10 days, the puppies will be able to shiver, aiding in their temperature regulation. The ear canals will begin to open, exposing the puppies to muffled sounds, and the eyelids may begin to separate, but the puppy will not have any vision. The eyelids open slowly, with some opening more rapidly than others. Do not force them open, as this may cause irreparable damage. Be patient; all will occur in time.

WEEK TWO

Weigh and worm the puppies according to each individual's body weight with a product such as Pyrantel Pamoate. The bitch should be wormed at the same intervals. All puppies are born with roundworms, which are contracted during the nursing process. Log the weight of each puppy on their individual records.

The ear canals should be open and the puppies may begin detecting sound. This can be seen by their reactions to sudden noises. Their eyes are opening and they can detect outlines and forms, but they cannot see clearly.

WEEK THREE

Weigh and worm the puppies and the bitch according to weight. Ensure that each puppy shows signs of weight gain. Begin feeding solid food by using the same food that is being fed to the bitch. Separate the bitch from the litter before feeding the puppies.

Pre-soften the food by adding a calf milk replacer to dry food until the food is floating. Allow the food to soak for four to six hours. Mash it into a soupy mixture and add water if necessary. Place each puppy by the food and allow them to eat as much as they want. If a puppy walks away before eating, place it by the dish, put a bit of food on your finger, and hold it so the puppy may lick it. As he licks your finger, lower it to the bowl and help him to eat. If any of them refuse to eat, do not be alarmed. You will be feeding them again and they may begin eating at the next feeding. Feed this mixture two to three times each day, but allow the puppies to continue to nurse.

Ear canals are fully functional. Eyelids should be open and the eyes visible. The puppies are able to see images, but cannot focus at this time. If the eyelids have not opened fully, you should seek veterinary advice.

This is the time to begin testing the hearing of each puppy. Hold each puppy and make a sound that the puppy is not accustomed to. You should see or feel an indication of the pup's ability to distinguish sound. You may feel the puppy react in a startled manner, or by watching the ears closely, you can see them twitch. Repeatedly using the same sound is ineffective, as the puppy will become accustomed to hearing it and ignore the sound. Any puppy that does not give some indication is suspect of being deaf. I use a tuning fork set at 1006 cycles for testing. Hit the fork on an object and hold it approximately three inches from each ear. The ear should move, giving an indication of hearing the sound. Holding the tuning fork too closely will allow the puppy to feel the vibrations and will give you a false indication.

WEEK FOUR

Weigh the puppies and ensure that they are gaining weight. Retest their hearing. Test the eyes by shining a penlight into each eye and observing the pupils' widening and narrowing. Ensure that the pupils are centered and without deformity. Pupils should be round and centered within the eye.

Continue adding the calf milk replacer to the dry food, but do not mash it. The puppies will take a little longer eating this for the first time, as they will need to chew more than with the mashed food. After the first day, there should not be any delays in eating.

WEEK FIVE

Weigh and worm the puppies and the bitch according to weight. Ensure that each puppy shows signs of weight gain. The puppies may begin eating dry food at this time. As with the wet food, it may take a little more time to consume the food and it may be messy, but once they get the idea of crunching and chewing, it will not take them long to finish.

If you are not absolutely certain that any puppy is capable of hearing from both ears, have them BAER tested by your vet. If you have not tested any of the puppies, they should all be BAER tested. While at the veterinarian's office, have their eyes checked as well.

WEEK SIX

Weigh and worm the puppies and the bitch according to weight. Ensure that each puppy shows signs of weight gain. Increase the amount of food being consumed, if needed.

This is the time to administer their first in the series of vaccinations. I prefer to give a seven-in-one shot. This provides protection against adenovirus 1 and 2, hepatitis, canine distemper, parainfluenza, leptospirosis, and parvovirus.

This is the earliest a puppy should leave the litter if the new owner is picking it up. Ensure that all puppies have their first series of vaccinations prior to leaving your facility.

WEEK EIGHT

This is the earliest that a puppy may be shipped to its new owner. Shipping a puppy, whether by air or land, requires a veterinary certificate of health that is not more than ten days old on the day of shipping.

From this point forward in the puppy's life, the vaccination schedule listed in the chapter "Diseases and Vaccines," page 73, should be followed.

Reproduction Problems

IF ovulation is correctly timed, reproduction should be expected, but if the timing is incorrect, there could be copulation without reproduction. This is the most common reason for the lack of reproduction. Listed below are some of the problems most commonly related to reproduction failure. There are many other less common causes of reproduction failure that are too numerous to list.

MALES

Balanoposthitis is an infection of the male's penis, including the glans and foreskin. This condition may be caused by a wound to the area or the invasion of foreign matter, and is normally accompanied by a greenish discharge and the dog's obsession with licking.

Cryptorchidism is the failure of one or both testicles to descend. This is an inherited trait, and a dog with even a single testicle should not be allowed to breed. The absent testicle remains inside the dog. Due to the higher incidence of cancer, he should be neutered.

Orchitis is inflammation, infection, and swelling of the testicles. This condition is very painful and is usually related to an infection of the epididymis that has spread to the testicles.

Brucellosis is a canine venereal disease that affects male sexual organs and female reproductive organs and can cause infertility in both. The disease is spread through contact with urine, feces, semen, vaginal discharge, aborted puppies, or other body secretions from an infected animal. There is no known cure for brucellosis and the majority of dogs that contract the disease are euthanized.

FEMALES

Dystocia refers to a difficult labor or insufficient uterine function. Oxytocin is usually prescribed in these cases, but it might be necessary to perform an emergency caesarean delivery.

Mastitis is an infection of the mammary glands and is accompanied by redness, swelling, tenderness, and pain. Milk that is not allowed to flow will thicken and block the mammary duct, causing this infection.

Persistent estrus, also known as prolonged estrus, is a condition where the bitch remains in estrus for 21 days or more. Failure to produce progesterone at the proper time may be the reason for a prolonged cycle. Other causes are follicular cysts, ovarian tumors, pituitary tumors, or liver disease.

Pseudopregnancy, more commonly referred to as false pregnancy, may be seen in a bitch that acts as if she is pregnant without actually being pregnant. This could be an ovarian problem, caused by progesterone.

Pyometra is a uterine infection that may be caused by hormonal changes or bacterial growth. During estrus, the cervix is open and susceptible to bacterial growth. Left untreated, this can result in death. Spaying is the only cure. Keeping the breeding area sanitary is the best possible prevention. Pyometra is more often seen in bitches that are not spayed or bred.

Silent heat occurs when the bitch goes through the estrus cycle without any outward signs of being in heat. There will be no swelling of the vulva or any bleeding present.

Split estrus occurs when a bitch enters proestrus and then fails to enter estrus, or has a very short estrus. Breeding at this time will usually fail; however, within 3 to 4 weeks, the bitch appears as if she is going into heat again. Breeding during this second cycle will generally result in reproduction. A bitch that consistently has split heats may have chronic premature luteolysis or hypothyroidism.

Vaginitis is a bacterial infection in the vagina. Left untreated, the infection can progress to the uterus and ovaries, causing infertility.

There is always the risk of a successful breeding being aborted by other causes such as illness, trauma, or medication. Care must be taken when administering any type of medication or treatment to a pregnant bitch, including annual vaccinations. Although considered safe, all vaccinations that are due while the bitch is pregnant should not be given until after the puppies are whelped.

Unplanned Breeding

There may come a time when a breeding takes place that is not planned or desired. When this occurs, there are two options available: either allow the litter to be whelped normally, or abort the litter. Allowing the litter to be whelped and placing the pups with desirable owners may be the best option, especially if you intend to use her for breeding in the future. If you prefer not to allow the litter to be whelped, aborting the litter is your other choice. There are two methods of abortion, surgical and chemical. These options may produce immediate results but can have undesirable consequences. Only you will be able to determine whether you have the ability or the will to accept those consequences.

First on the list of aborting a litter of puppies is to have an ovariohysterectomy, which means removal of the fetus and spaying the bitch at the same time. Obviously, if you intend to breed in the future, it is better to whelp the litter and place the puppies in new homes.

There is a variety of pharmaceuticals referred to as litter avoidance drugs, which may cause the abortion or absorption of an unwanted litter without the use of invasive surgery. These drugs are not approved for use on dogs. There are a number of side effects that are deemed serious enough to reject their use.

Most of the recommendations provided are to give the medication while the dog is still in estrus. Doing this prolongs the estrus cycle, keeping the males interested in breeding, and she could become pregnant again. There are other considerations, however. The medication can increase the risk of pyometra, which can only be cured by spaying. Temporary sterility could inhibit pregnancy for as much as two to three years, or if there is a successful pregnancy, the litter size may be dramatically reduced.

Although there are proponents of this method who maintain that it is be safe, it has been my experience that the use of abortive drugs should be avoided, especially if you intend to use the bitch for breeding in the future. My advice would be to allow her to have the litter and simply to care for the puppies as you would have a planned litter. Place the puppies in pet homes along with a spay or neuter agreement. It is not worth the risk of ruining a brood bitch with procedures that can do more harm than good.

Afterword

In closing, I hope that this book has achieved its purpose of providing the reader with the factual information about the history and care of this unique breed. There were many hours of research poured into obtaining these historical facts and yet, there remains a cloud of mystery.

For those who are intent on breeding, I hope that those chapters become a part of your program and you endeavor to produce the best possible breeding, regardless of the time or cost. Keep in mind that there are many other books on this subject and you should make as many of them available to you as possible.

To those who own this fantastic breed as a pet, please remember that this is a working dog, and exercise of their mind and bodies are important. A lack of exercise can make a dog anxious, leading to destructive behaviors.

In my mind's eye this is a breed that we have been blessed with, and every effort should be made to keep it as it was meant to be. Although working in the sense that it was originally intended is dying out, there are many other areas to keep them active. Please don't allow this breed to be ruined.

Please visit my website at http://www.abneycatahoulas.com and if you would like to comment on the book or its contents you may email me at don@abneycatahoulas.com

About the Author

Don Abney was introduced to dogs at an early age when his father, while on a hunting trip, caught and brought home a wild puppy. It was the training of this puppy by Don and his father that inspired him to become a dog trainer. Many years would pass before he realized that he had a talent for training and put it to use by establishing Abney Canine Training.

His love for Catahoulas and his dream of breeding them came true when he moved to Abita Springs, Louisiana. There he met Vernon Traxler, an old-time breeder, who helped him establish his kennel, Abney Catahoulas, and became his mentor in the breeding of Catahoulas.

With this dream fulfilled, he ventured into the realm of search and rescue. There were no groups or teams listed as working in the area, so he contacted the local sheriff's office. Major Bill Dobson directed him to a couple of ladies working with a pair of dogs in and around St. Tammany Parish. At first, they were reluctant to accept a Catahoula, because their only knowledge of the breed was that it was a good hog dog. After proving himself and his dog, Ladyhawke, a bond was established with them. As more dog teams began to arrive, the decision was made to establish the Louisiana Search and Rescue dog group. As a founding member, trainer, and its treasurer, Don set forth to have LaSAR established as a 501(c)(3) nonprofit organization.

Prior to his involvement in search and rescue, Don worked for Southern Bell Telephone Company, later known as Bellsouth, where he spent 30 years working as an electronic technician, and then retired. During this time, in addition to working in SAR, he became a deputy with the St. Tammany Parish sheriff's office. He worked for 13 years in special operations and attained the rank of lieutenant prior to retiring from that field.

Below is a list of his accomplishments:
- Master trainer in obedience, tracking, hunting, search and rescue, and detector dogs since 1980

- Court-certified expert in the field of canine training and tracking through the criminal district courts of New Orleans, Louisiana, December 10, 1998, by Judge Julian Parker
- United Kennel Club (UKC) Conformation & Junior Showmanship judge
- American Kennel Club (AKC) Canine Good Citizen (CGC) evaluator
- Coauthor of bill signed into the Louisiana legislature presenting CGC as a dog-defensive law
- Member of the Association of Pet Dog Trainers (APDT)
- Licensed by the Drug Enforcement Agency as a researcher in the field of canine training, 1992
- Studied and trained in dog psychology, animal behavior, breeding and genetics, and canine nutrition and health care
- Trained and experienced in handling dangerous, vicious, and nuisance animals since 1994 with a commendation from the St. Tammany Parish sheriff's office
- Presenter of Hug a Tree and Survive, a survivor program for youths lost in the wilderness
- Developer and presenter of the Lost and Safe Program, designed to keep children safe when lost in the wilderness, urban, and shopping centers, as well as computer safety and stranger awareness
- Founding member and trainer of Louisiana Search and Rescue Dogs, Inc., 1989–1996
- Member of the National Association of Search and Rescue, 1989–2000
- Retired Lieutenant, St. Tammany Parish Sheriff's Office, Search and Rescue Division
- Owner, handler, and trainer of Ladyhawke, the first registered Louisiana Catahoula certified in search and rescue and narcotics detection and commissioned by law enforcement. She received the first Service Champion Award for outstanding work in community service, presented by the National Association of Louisiana Catahoulas (NALC).
- Recipient of the Excellence in Training award presented by Sigma Chemical Corporation
- Author of *The Louisiana Catahoula Leopard Dog*, a book on the history, breeding, and care of Louisiana Catahoulas
- Author of *The Abney Method to Owning a Dog*, a book on care and maintenance, behaviors, first aid, and choosing and training a dog

- Author of *Canine Tracking Guide*, a book on choosing and training a dog for human, animal, competition, and blood tracking, including care and maintenance, and first aid
- Certified breeder of registered Louisiana Catahoula Leopard Dogs since 1985 (NALC)
- Past president of the American Catahoula Association
- Vice-president of the Great Southern Kennel Club, a UKC organization, 2003–2007
- President of the Great Southern Kennel Club, 2007–2008
- Founder and president of the Catahoula Owners, Breeders, and Research Association (COBRA), 2004–present
- Director, Lost Souls, a canine organization formed to aid law enforcement and individuals in the investigation of unresolved cold cases.

Bibliography

Battagilia, Carmelo L., PhD, *Breeding Better Dogs.* Georgia: BEI Publications, Inc., 1995.

Brisbin, Jr., I. Lehr, Ph.D, *Wolves and Related Canids.* University of Georgia, Savannah River Ecology Lab, 1992.

Byington, Cyrus, *The Dictionary of the Choctaw Language.* Washington, DC: Government Printing Office, 1915.

Catahoula Parish Court House, Catahoula Parish History, 2003.

Centers for Disease Control and Prevention, photos of ticks and Giardia. Atlanta, Georgia: 2008.

Clark, L.A., PhD, et al., "Canine SINEs and their effects on phenotypes of the domestic dog." In: *Genomics of Disease.* New York: Springer Science+Business Media, LLC (2008), J.P. Gustafson, J. Taylor, G. Stacey, eds. 79-88.

Clayton, Lawrence A., et al., *The De Soto Chronicles: The Expedition of Hernando De Soto to North America 1539-1543.* Alabama: University of Alabama Press, 1994.

Crockford, Susan Janet, PhD., *Native Dog Types In North America before Arrival of European Dogs.* Victoria, BC, Canada: Pacific Identifications, Inc.

Cushman, H. B., *History of the Choctaw, Chickasaw, and Natchez Indians.* Texas: Headlight Printing House, 1899.

Dzanis, David A., DVM, PhD, DACVN, "Interpreting Pet Food Labels," United States Food and Drug Administration (2007), Center for Veterinary Medicine.

Gagliano, Sherwood M. and Hiram F. Gregory, Jr., "A preliminary survey of Paleo-Indian points from Louisiana." *Louisiana Studies* (1965), 4(1):62-77.

Gayarré, Charles E., *History of Louisiana, The French Domination.* New York: Redfield, 1854.

Gregory, Hiram F., Jr., "Eighteenth century Caddoan archaeology: a study in models and interpretation." Unpublished Ph.D. thesis. Dallas, Texas: Department of Anthropology, Southern Methodist University, 1974.

Gregory, Hiram E., Jr. and Clarence H. Webb, "European trade beads from six sites in Natchitoches Parish, Louisiana." *Florida Anthropologist* (1965), 18(3): 1544.

Goertz, John W. et. al., "The Status of Wild Canis in Louisiana." *American Midland Naturalist*, Vol. 93, No. 1 (January 1975), 215-218, published by University of Notre Dame.

Iljin, N.A., "Wolf-dog genetics." *Journal of Genetics* (1944) 42:359-414.

Kniffen, Fred B., Gregory, Hiram F., Stokes, George A., *The Historic Indian Tribes of Louisiana, From 1542 to Present*. Louisiana State University Press, 1994.

Little, Clarence C., ScD, *The Inheritance of Coat Color in Dogs*. New York: Howell Book House, 1957.

Onstott, Phillip, *The New Art of Breeding Better Dogs*. New York: Howell Book House, 1968.

Padgett, George A., DVM, *Control of Canine Genetic Diseases*. New York: Howell Book House, 1998.

Page, Thomas, *The Civilization of the American Indian*. Geneva, Switzerland: Minerva, 1979.

Reed, Ann L. et al. "Effect of dam and sire qualitative hip conformation scores on progeny hip conformation." *Journal of the American Veterinary Medical Association* (September 1, 2000), Vol. 217, No. 5, 675-680.

Ruvinsky, A., and Sampson, J., *The Genetics of the Dog*. New York: CABI Publishing, 2001.

Strain, George M., PhD, et al., "Deafness prevalence in dogs heterozygous or homozygous for the merle allele." *Journal of Veterinary Internal Medicine* (2009), 23:282-286.

Swanton, John R., *Indian Tribes Of The Lower Mississippi Valley And Adjacent Coast Of The Gulf Of Mexico*, Washington, D.C.: Government Printing Office, 1911.

Taensa Indian Tribe History, *Handbook of American Indians,* 1906.

Willis, Malcolm B., *Genetics of the Dog*. New York: Howell Book House, 1989.

Wymond, John, *in Louisiana Historical Quarterly,* Louisiana: Louisiana Historical Society, 1917.

Young, Stanley P., and Edward A. Goldman, *Wolves of North America*. Dover Publications Inc., 1944.

Printed by BoD™in Norderstedt, Germany